DR MIKE SMITH'S

POSTBAG

BACK PAIN

WITH SHARRON KERR

KYLE CATHIE LIMITED

First published 1993 by
Kyle Cathie Limited
3 Vincent Square
London SW1P 2LX

ISBN 1 85626 088 7

A CIP catalogue record for this title
is available from the British Library

Typeset by DP Photosetting, Aylesbury, Bucks
Printed and bound in Great Britain by
Butler & Tanner Ltd, Frome and London

CONTENTS

INTRODUCTION

I always feel the ironic thing about back problems is that so often they are avoidable. Yet, at any one time, around one and a half million people in this country are suffering from some degree of back trouble – from hairdressers, builders, decorators, nurses, newsagents (just think of the bundles of newspapers they lift daily), to tennis players like Boris Becker and polo players like the Prince of Wales. Back pain seems to rival the common cold in costs to British industry, and headaches as a reason for visiting the doctor.

On any one day, at least 88,000 people are likely to be off work with back pain. In fact, around sixty million working days are lost each year because of it, and that's not counting the odd day or two off work as a result of over-strenuous gardening or because you rearranged the living-room furniture yet again!

Such is the cost to industry that in the United States even insurance companies are taking an interest in the monitoring and treatment of back problems. At an American university, a team has been researching various aspects of back pain, including looking at the possibility of producing an early warning device that triggers an alarm if the user over-exerts his or her back muscles. The device is a spin-off from the team's research into ways of measuring the severity of the most common form of back problem – low back pain. Their method is called electromyography, the measurement of electrical activity in the complex web of back muscles as they contract.

Back problems are one of the biggest causes of ill health, producing a demoralising sequence of pain, poor mobility, sleeplessness and, in extreme cases, depression. Back pain is rarely something that can be ignored and is a problem that doesn't always provoke the sympathy and understanding that it should – probably because pain is such a subjective thing, and also because back problems can be so varied and complex: from a mild, irritable ache, to uncomfortable stiffness, to such agonising, fierce pain the sufferer can't even stand up straight. The extreme pain that comes as a result of a back problem is difficult to imagine if you've never suffered from it. It can be very distressing – even more so if you're on your own when the pain first comes on. It can be frightening to find yourself stuck in a set position or experience pain so intense you want to vomit. (Before you become too alarmed, I have to say that the good news is that most back pain will be better within a month, often less.)

Time and again back pain interrupts every facet of daily life and can be so debilitating that sufferers cannot work – or play, for that matter.

According to the National Back Pain Association, in 1990 an amazing 34 million people, that's two out of every three people in the UK, suffered from back pain. The worrying point about a figure such as this is that the incidence of back pain seems to be getting worse – some studies suggest that it's doubled in the last decade or so – possibly due to increasingly sedentary lifestyles. It's even been said that these days British backs are beginning to be as stiff as our upper lips!

THE COMMON CAUSES OF BACK PAIN

YOUR BACK

It's not easy to appreciate how back problems arise without first understanding the nature of our backbone, a major part of the remarkable piece of natural engineering that is the skeletal system. The spine can be described as the centre of the body and for some people the cause of more trouble than any other part of the skeleton. It's put under stress when you stand up, bend, turn, swivel, carry, lift and so on.

The spine stretches from the bottom of your skull to your buttocks. It's also known as the vertebral column and it is made up of twenty-four vertebrae and 110 joints. The vertebrae can be divided into the top seven cervical vertebrae – the most mobile part of the spine; the middle twelve thoracic vertebrae, also known as the dorsal section, where each vertebra has a rib attached on each side; and the lower five lumbar vertebrae, with the sacrum (five fused vertebrae in a triangular shape) and coccyx at the tail end of the spine. The firm sacrum gives extra strength and stability to the pelvis, which is essential for the attachments of the muscles, fibres and ligaments that span the hollow pelvis to form its base and which support the weight of all the organs and tissues within the abdomen. The coccyx is merely a remnant of the tail possessed by our animal ancestors. To look at the spine from the front or back you'd naturally assume it was a straight structure. In fact, viewed from the side, you'll notice that it has four gentle curves from the top to the bottom.

The vertebrae surround and protect the spinal cord – the main means of nerve communication between all parts of the body and the brain. There's a network of nerves, each one linked to the spinal cord between the vertebrae.

Intevertebral discs lie between each vertebra. These flat cartilages (tough, elastic tissue) cushion the vertebrae as the spine moves, helping to give it its vast range of movement. They also serve as shock absorbers which protect the spine from damage.

A complicated network of muscles and ligaments holds everything together and keeps the spine stable but flexible. At the root of the potential problem is the fact that these muscles of the spine are not able to work as efficiently as muscles elsewhere in the body. Scientists call this a mechanical disadvantage. These tiny muscles have to remain taut and have very little room for manoeuvre. So under undue strain they are more likely to tear rather than stretch.

Simple wear and tear is one theory for the cause of back pain, but it could also be that the human spine was designed to be horizontal and back trouble started when man stood up. Though experts disagree over this, some believe that since we stood up on our hind legs, the added stress the spine has to bear makes it vulnerable to strain and injury. Aeons of years of evolution haven't been able to compensate us for this conversion, so extra stress is placed on the spine, particularly the neck and back areas which are not supported by the rib cage.

However backs can play up because of injury to bones, perhaps through a fall or fracture, and by joints and ligaments being damaged, as well as damage to muscles and tendons.

STRAINS, SPRAINS AND INJURIES

I'm always being asked about the most common cause of back pain. First of all, back pain describes all manner of pain on the back surface of the body – from the occiput (the back part of the skull) to the coccyx (the small bone at the bottom of the spinal column). As few as 3 per cent of back problems are due to extraspinal or spinal disease – an inflamed central nervous system with meningitis, for instance, or the upper back pain of kidney disease. The remainder are usually lumbosacral back pain of muscoskeletal origin and most back problems occur in the area of the five lumbar vertebrae in the lower back.

Back pain in the lumbar region is sometimes referred to as lumbago and the most common cause is a sprain, strain or tear in one of the ligaments – which help to hold the spine together – or in one of the back muscles. (Upper back pain can also be caused by weak muscles or strains and sprains.) Usually the pain of a sprain or strain eases within a week or so with a combination of bed rest and painkillers.

The lumbar region is commonly called the small of the back – the small inward curve at the base of the spine. It's here that we pivot forward when we bend from the waist like a crane, and here that most of the weight of the head and upper body is borne when we do so. It's not surprising, is it, that this region is where most problems arise?

To try to comprehend why we place so much strain on our spines, all you have to do is run through in your mind your total movements from the moment you wake up to the moment you go to sleep. Have you ever counted the number of times you bend forward in a day? I'm sure you'll be surprised at the number of flexion movements you make, from leaning over when answering the phone, to turning on taps, taking something out of the fridge, tying shoelaces, dressing a young child, putting babies into car seats or picking things up from the floor (which most of us do incorrectly, without bending from the knees).

But really, it's not just bending that causes back problems, it's any activity that puts an undue strain on the back – especially bending and twisting at the same time – for example, lifting a load from the ground and putting it on to a shelf at the side of you at head height. More generally, back problems can start with any sudden new activity, such as a frenzied burst of DIY; gardening, including such repetitive work as weeding; golfing; skiing or a game of tennis when you haven't played for some time.

Or it could be an activity that isn't so new – hours

hunched over a desk or at a typewriter, particularly if the chair you sit on gives inadequate support and throws a great strain on the back. Sitting or standing too long in bad positions can often cause problems.

A very common cause of back pain is a mechanical failure of some part of the structure of the spine leading to a bone becoming slightly displaced. This usually stems from an awkward movement which puts extra strain on the spine, but it can also be caused by an injury. The bones in the spine can be fractured and damaged after a fall or in an accident or car crash. Whiplash is quite a common injury sustained in even the most minor of car accidents, for example.

Most of the time low back pain is due to weak muscles, bad posture or being overweight but it, too, can be caused by injury to the sacrum or coccyx, more often than not as a result of suddenly sitting down on something hard, which can cause a great deal of pain. The pain can become even worse when the person is seated which makes it a very awkward injury. Pain in the coccyx seems to be far more common in women but no one knows quite why. This type of injury can cause pain for a very long time. I've often received queries about this in my postbag, particularly when someone has fallen heavily and fractured the coccyx and is still in pain some eighteen months later.

Such an injury can be very difficult to treat and some sufferers may find they have to try a whole range of procedures – such as osteopathy or physiotherapy, which I discuss later – before they find something that helps. And, unfortunately, the pain can still come back despite bouts of relief at the time of treatment.

The source of the pain is often the nerves around the coccyx, rather than the damaged tissues resulting from a fracture. Doctors have found that, in severe cases, the nerve pain can continue even when the coccyx – in desperation to produce relief – is removed by surgery.

So often people 'abuse' their back for years. They constantly ignore aches and pains, which sometimes act as early warning signals, and carry on gardening without using knee-mats, or wallpapering for too many hours at a time even though their back is aching, or lifting things incorrectly because they can't be bothered to bend from the knees. Therefore, frequently a problem has been building up for years, and has often been ignored. Ignored, that is, until the back suddenly 'goes' during a minor action such as bending down or even sneezing.

Mike, a thirty-six-year-old marketing executive, who had played rugby for more than twenty years no matter how many muscles in his back were aching, was suddenly confined to bed for three days after merely leaning over the bathroom washbasin to brush his teeth.

It came totally out of the blue, although I'd had various back pains in the past. Usually it was just a case of occasional stiffness. Stiff, aching muscles on a Sunday following a game on the Saturday. I also found that if I drove for long distances my back would ache but it would always go away overnight and never stop me participating in any games. So I'd get aches and pains because of strains after exercising or driving – certainly not serious enough to seek medical help.

I'd read that the average motorist can spend two weeks a year just driving. I probably spend a lot more time than that because of the driving I have to do as a matter of course in my job which takes me all over the country visiting clients. I'm also quite tall so it's difficult for me to find a comfortable driving position. It's impossible to drive with my legs completely outstretched, or my arms for that matter.

But on this particular morning, I didn't even feel any kind of ache or strain. I got up, had a shower and went to brush my teeth. As I leaned over the sink the whole of my middle to lower back suddenly seized up with one enormous muscular spasm. It made me lean on to the sink and collapse on to my knees. When the spasm eased after a few seconds, I remember thinking that the only similar experience I'd had before that was bad cramp in my legs. The difference was that after the cramp had worn off I had no pain, but when the spasm in my back had ended I was still left with muscle pain in my back.

I couldn't tell what was causing the pain, it was so intense, I couldn't distinguish whether it was a trapped nerve or a pulled muscle. I was really puzzled by the incident because I didn't expect someone of my age, who was doing regular exercise, to have back problems. I thought it must be a sign of old age a few decades early!

Mike struggled back to his bedroom to lie down for a short while because he was still convinced that the pain was temporary and he'd be able to go to work as normal.

I couldn't find a comfortable position. I tried to move around slightly to find the least painful position. In the end the only way I could lie was flat on my back with my knees up. I had no choice but to stay put because I couldn't move around anyway. Going to the loo was a major problem. As soon as I'd leave my comfortable position I would get sharp pains in my back again as I moved and tried to walk to the bathroom.

Having to lie in bed for three days was very frustrating, particularly when I could only lie in one position. The thought of a long, hot soak in the bath was tempting to try to ease my backache but the pain was so bad I couldn't even do that.

On the fourth day there had been quite a dramatic improvement overnight but I did still feel I needed treatment. I was pleased that I was now mobile enough to see a physiotherapist. She thought I'd pulled a muscle which put pressure on a nerve, which was why I was in such pain and why it was so awkward to find a comfortable position. She gave me infra-red heat treatment and massage which was like being in heaven it was so soothing.

She explained that often people get up in the morning without stretching properly and then by immediately leaning over the sink you put your back under enormous strain. So since then I've taken care to have a good stretch when I wake up before I even get out of bed. Even if I oversleep I make a point of not jumping out of bed in a rush and not doing a lot of sudden movements like bending over the bathroom sink so quickly. Basically your body needs limbering up in the morning just as it does before you do any kind of exercise.

SCIATICA

Sciatica is one of the most common forms of low back pain. It is an inflammation of the sciatic nerve – the largest nerve in the body. As this nerve leaves its several roots between the vertabrae in the lower back, it looks like many railway lines leaving a large city terminus and becoming funnelled into a two-track line. There's a sciatic nerve on both sides of the body, going down the back of each leg.

Sciatica is most commonly triggered by bending from the waist instead of from the knees, particularly when lifting a heavy object and twisting the body at the same time. This can strain or sprain the ligaments holding the vertebrae together, for example, or perhaps cause the intervertebral discs to become squashed, so that they burst and their soft inner core bulges out, pressing on the sciatic nerve as it leaves the spine. In the first case, the congestion of the tissues can cause pain; in the second, the protruding disc can press upon the nerve so hard that it first causes pain, then loss of sensation in the leg; and it may eventually lead to loss of movement in one or both legs.

The pain of sciatica can be felt anywhere along the line of the sciatic nerve – most often in the lower back (usually the buttock), down the back of the thigh, or front of the leg. Sufferers describe it as a continuous drilling, even jangling kind of intense pain. In severe cases, people are so totally overwhelmed with such pain that normal daily life comes to an abrupt halt.

Godfrey, a sixty-two-year-old retired director, had not only been lifting heavy pieces of equipment at his engineering company in the days before the sudden onset of sciatica, but he'd also been doing some DIY at home when he fell awkwardly.

> I was up a ladder painting the main living-room ceiling when the ladder gave way. As I was holding a pot of white paint at the time all I could think of was not getting paint on any furniture or on the carpet rather than any damage I might do to myself.
>
> So I fell really awkwardly backwards on to the hard corner of the sofa with my arms outstretched hanging on to the paint pot. I'm glad to say I saved the paint and then didn't think any more about the pain in the lower part of my back.
>
> About a week later, I was starting to get extremely bad pains in my lower back and down into my leg. It was as if a red-hot poker was stuck into the middle of my left leg. The pain was continuous, a stabbing, knife-like pain. I wasn't sure what on earth it was at that point. The pain in my back was so bad I even thought it was some kind of kidney infection such was its intensity.

Godfrey stuck the pain for two weeks, but as it was getting increasingly severe rather than subsiding he finally sought the help of his GP.

> He told me straight away that I had an inflamed sciatic nerve. He said that rest was the best cure for

it – something that I had not been having the way I was trying to soldier on.

I gave in and stayed in bed for two weeks. I was frightened into it more than anything else because my leg went completely numb. It was a horrible sensation, as if I was going to be permanently paralysed. And after that any move I made was very painful, especially in my left heel. I also had pins and needles in my heel, too.

The pain did ease with rest but it continued off and on for about three months. It always seemed to be lurking in the background. I particularly noticed the problem when I was driving or getting in and out of the car. So much for saving the furniture and carpet from damage!

Once you've had an attack of sciatica following an injury, you are more likely to have further problems, especially if your job is a physical one where you may strain your back again.

Sol, a twenty-eight-year-old mother, first had sciatic pain three years ago while she was working as a travel agent and again recently when she was pregnant with her first child. She believes the cause of the intense pain was lifting heavy bundles of holiday brochures incorrectly.

We were clearing a room full of holiday brochures and I was lifting bundles of them. A couple of days afterwards I noticed a twinge in my buttocks when I stood up after sitting down. It didn't hurt at any other time but soon got so noticeable that I had to put my hand on my lower back as I stood up.

The pain gradually intensified and then began to radiate down her left leg.

The pain was now very sharp. It hurt most when I stood up and for the first few steps I took. I couldn't walk very far even so because my left leg felt very heavy. Then my lower back began to hurt constantly and in the end I couldn't move. I had to stay in bed for a week which helped a little but not very much.

My doctor told me that I had a muscle spasm that affected the sciatic nerve which was causing the pain in my buttocks and down my leg.

Sol had no idea when she hurt her back that the pain would last for so long as it did or that it would be quite so disabling.

I needed physiotherapy to try to relieve the pain and I had a massage on my back which was very pleasant and did help a little. I had a massage every day for a week. I was told not to lift heavy objects, not to bend unless I bent my knees and that I shouldn't lean over to lift anything.

A common complaint from people who suffer from back pain is the lack of understanding they experience, particularly from colleagues if they have had to have extended time off work. Sol was no exception.

I had six weeks off work but didn't have much sympathy when I went back and said that I couldn't lift anything heavy. As a travel agent lifting heavy manuals is unavoidable, as well as lifting bundles of brochures.

Some of the other staff were pretty resentful that I wouldn't do any lifting because we all were supposed to do it. They thought I looked OK so why was I avoiding things? They thought I was trying to get privileged treatment and that I was putting it all on because I didn't want to do that part of the job.

Such was the resentment, in fact, that Sol's only way

round this was to get a note from her doctor to say that she couldn't lift heavy objects.

Also, to her surprise, despite taking time off work, having physiotherapy and resting properly, the pain took quite a long time to disappear completely – two years in all. The sciatica problem didn't go away entirely either, which was another shock. The trouble resurfaced when she was pregnant.

> I was fine all the way through the pregnancy until the last month. Apparently, the baby was lying in the position where it was affecting the sciatic nerve. The pain wasn't bad all the time, just when I tried to put down my left leg to walk. I had to limp with the help of crutches.
>
> Doctors thought they might have to induce me if the pain was too bad but decided that as long as I wasn't too badly affected there was no need to do that. They also told me to try to manage without painkillers which I did. I felt uncomfortable as it was at the end of the pregnancy but this problem just made me feel even more uncomfortable. Limping is pretty difficult when you're that heavy!

Fortunately, sciatic pain that can come on in late pregnancy, whether you've suffered before or not, should go with the delivery as the baby is no longer pressing on the nerves. Resting flat on your bed is usually the only way to bring relief meanwhile.

SLIPPED DISCS

The normal wear and tear of the ageing process, poor posture, muscular tension and bad working habits can all contribute to back pain, and doctors will also take into account weight, age and occupation when looking for a cause. The mechanical causes of back pain can be due to one of a wide range of factors, as I've said – strains and tears of muscles and ligaments or an injury to the tiny facet joints of the vertebrae – but can also be due to a rupture of the outer layers of the disc, commonly called a slipped disc.

Not only is the term 'slipped disc' misleading, so is the condition. When people suddenly develop a back problem, friends invariably comment, 'You've probably slipped a disc,' imagining the disc to be shaped like a tap washer. In fact, these intervertebral discs are strongly attached to the side of each vertebra, as I explained earlier, and contrary to popular belief it is impossible for them to slip. So, as they don't slip out, they can't, as so many people might imagine, be popped back into position.

Each year approximately one in two hundred people suffer the severe pain of a prolapsed disc, to use the correct term.

To understand how a disc prolapses, you need to understand the make-up of the back's discs. These discs, of which there are twenty-three, have a semi-liquid, jelly-like centre, or nucleus, and a tough fibrous outer casing called the annulus. In other words, they are like flat, spongy cushions between the bony vertebrae and have soft centres rather like sofa cushions. They act in a similar way to ballbearings or shock absorbers whenever the spine moves. However, when subjected to too much stress they 'burst' (prolapse) enabling some of the soft inner pulp to leak out or bulge (herniate), pressing on surrounding nerves and tissues and causing great pain. The area where most slipped discs occur is in the lumbar region since these endure the most strain – although any disc is at risk of prolapsing.

Discs are tough and hardwearing during childhood and adolescence and problems are uncommon under the age of twenty-five or so. However, in time, minor injuries, repetitive stresses and just getting older can lead to splits and fissures in the outer casing and a gradual weakening of the disc. (But please don't worry needlessly, normally a great deal of wear and tear must have gone on before a disc prolapses.) When this occurs the disc's outer layers, or 'walls', are weakened and the back may feel stiff for a few days. It can then be something quite minor, perhaps a cough, a sneeze, or a sudden twisting movement, that finally ruptures the disc walls.

As the discs don't contain any nerves the pain is due to pressure from the bulging disc – or fragments of it – on nearby nerves. The intensity of the pain and the occurrence of other symptoms depends on which nerves are affected. This is due to such great pressure being exerted on the nerve that it isn't able to 'instruct' the muscle to move properly.

The resulting symptoms are at best pain, or at worse paralysis of the lower leg. The sciatic nerve, for example, as I've explained, provides a nervous supply to the legs and is based in the lumbar region. So pressure on this nerve can cause pain or other sensations in the legs.

Simple rest is helpful. Something as basic as putting a board under the mattress, unless you have a firm one already, or placing the mattress on the floor, will help speed recovery by giving the rigid flatness needed to prevent the painful tissues from sagging even further. In addition painkillers can be taken at regular intervals (see pages 51–5 for more details). Most cases do get better with straightforward treatment but the weakness and the risk of another attack remains. It's even thought that as many as nine out of ten cases of prolapsed discs would heal on their own in time without any treatment.

Nurses, and others with jobs involving constant lifting, are unfortunately often at risk of disc problems. So are lorry drivers and people who do a lot of driving, which has a tendency to jar the spine. Lack of exercise, which means that supporting muscles are weakened, and being overweight also increase your chances of a disc prolapse. This most often happens at the age of forty to forty-five. After fifty it's unusual for a disc to rupture. Beyond middle age the discs gradually harden and flatten, which could provide one of the answers to why we seem to get shorter as we get older. This, in itself, could cause back problems since the nerves leaving the vertebrae have less room, and so are more subject to pressure from movement of the spine. However 'shrinkage' in later years is usually due to the 'thinning' of the bones caused by osteoporosis (see page 24).

Joyce, a fifty-one-year-old retired nurse, found her back problems began in her twenties when she worked in a factory and her job involved lifting heavy weights. Like so many sufferers, she had an interval of many years before the problem resurfaced with a vengeance.

> I was working in a shellfish factory at the time. As I lifted some cans my back suddenly went, as people say. It's funny to think that at the time I didn't even realise the damage I was causing to my back and that I'd face years of pain and discomfort because of it.
>
> I just thought I'd strained my back and that if I ignored it, it would go away even though the pain was pretty severe.

Three days later Joyce was in such terrible pain she couldn't even get out of bed and once she was up she couldn't stand without help. 'I couldn't do anything the pain was so bad. It was frightening because I didn't expect that straining your back could cause such pain and I didn't know what to do.'

Her doctor also diagnosed a muscle strain. Yet for twelve months Joyce suffered with intermittent pain in her lower back.

> Some days were worse than others. There were days when I could move about and others when I couldn't move at all. After a few months I began to have pain in my left leg as well, which was like a throbbing, rampant toothache. Nothing would ease the pain apart from the short relief I got from taking painkillers. Walking became more difficult. I'd be

doubled up in pain. I couldn't straighten my back and I started having to drag one leg.

Eighteen months after first hurting her back Joyce was finally told by doctors that she had indeed suffered a disc prolapse – two of them. She was admitted to hospital for three weeks where she had traction and physiotherapy treatment to relieve the absolutely agonising pain she was in.

The traction did help relieve the pain. I lay flat on my back with my left leg in the air with weights at the end. I could literally feel the pressure being lessened after an hour or so on traction.

I also had manipulation therapy each morning. I lay on my stomach and the physiotherapist would rock her fingers back and forth on painful spots. This would be followed by great pain as if someone had kicked me in the back. But after six treatments it did ease the pain.

After treatment Joyce was told that one of the discs was still protruding and that the only option was surgery – a laminectomy (see page 60–61).

I was warned that, in my case, it could cure me or it could make me worse off. I decided not to risk it and was put in a plaster case from my neck to the tops of my legs for about six months. It was uncomfortable but it did ease the pain. It kept my back rigid and took any strain off it. As far as I was concerned it was the lesser of two evils. I made it more comfortable by pouring lots of talcum powder down into it to soak up any moisture. I wore trousers and loose tops to try to disguise it.

I'd have to roll in and out of bed. My husband used to help dress me. He'd have to put on my underwear and my tights. I couldn't have a bath so to wash myself I used to use a dish mop and I'd dry myself by putting a towel around it. Sometimes I felt as if there was no end in sight, and I would feel quite hopeless.

When I finally had the cast taken off it was such a relief. It was also a relief to find that the pain had got much better. I was aware that I had back trouble but I wasn't in pain. I wore surgical corsets which gave me support. I had a board under my mattress which I still have today.

Nowadays, a plaster case – or cast – is used only rarely. The modern equivalent is made of polystyrene, so is much lighter and can be taken off and put back on easily.

Joyce had no more problems until two years ago, after she had been working on a demanding psychogeriatric ward for many years.

I don't know exactly what caused my back trouble to re-occur. I suppose once you have had a 'slipped disc' you could be at risk of more back trouble if you're not careful. But at times I'm sure my job must have added to any strain. We'd have to try to dress patients, for example, and it would be quite a struggle because often they wouldn't want to get dressed.

The pain started to come back very gradually over a period of two months. This time it also affected my right leg, not my left. Again I thought it would go away if I ignored it. But it became so painful I couldn't. I couldn't put any weight on my leg and I finally had to give up work because of the pain.

Joyce has since found temporary relief in physiotherapy as well as by taking painkillers. She has learned to adapt her lifestyle so as not to aggravate her back. Like many people with back problems, she realises the importance of not putting a strain on your spine by lifting things incorrectly or by not thinking of how you might be damaging it through everyday actions.

It's now something I think about all the time. I'm careful about how I sit. I prefer an upright chair. I don't attempt to lift anything. A leaning or stretching forward movement starts the pain up again so I find I can only vacuum-clean in short bursts. I just do one room at a time, for example.

I find standing in queues difficult. If I stand for any length of time in one position, I have a numbness in my hip which then makes my whole leg go numb. It's a horrible sensation as if my leg isn't going to hold me and I'm going to fall over. So now I always try to go shopping with my daughter so that if we have to queue I can walk away if I feel the numbness starting. When my back is playing up I find a hot bath soothing although I make sure I have one when my daughter is around – otherwise I can't get out of the bath very well.

I also can't sit in a car for long journeys. Driving, too, has become more difficult because pressing down on the foot pedals puts a strain on my back.

I try to ignore my back problem as much as I can while at the same time realising that I have to be careful and not be too adventurous. That way I can live with it.

Unlike Joyce, whose discs prolapsed without any prior warning, Susan, thirty-nine, who works at an animal rescue centre, had years of niggling back pain before it culminated in a disc prolapse. And also unlike Joyce, Susan opted for surgery to relieve her problem.

The problem began roughly ten years ago. I don't know exactly what triggered it. I just kept getting painful twinges across the lower part of my back –

more uncomfortable niggles than severe pain. My doctor referred me to a rheumatologist who told me everything was in order and there was no reason why I was getting these pains. That made me feel a bit hopeless really, but I thought that specialists ought to know what they're talking about so didn't think much more of it. But gradually the pain got worse depending on the things I did.

Looking back I can see that I was doing a combination of all the wrong things. We were doing up a house and I would lift a wheelbarrow full of bricks, for instance, yet there was no particular incident that definitely triggered the pain. I've been asked by osteopaths and chiropractors whether I've ever had a fall. I did when I was much younger and I used to ride. They were never serious enough for me to be taken to hospital or to the doctor so I don't know whether they had anything to do with the origination of my back problems.

For more than five years Susan went back and forth to her doctor, to osteopaths and to chiropractors, who were good at relieving the pain, but the discomfort in her lower back would always return. To avoid aggravating the problem Susan even developed a strange way of walking. 'My sister described me as looking like a crab. I'd drop one shoulder to the side when I walked. When I stood completely straight and upright it would just make the pain worse!'

The 'crunch' finally came, unfortunately for Susan and her husband, at the start of a seven-week holiday of a lifetime to Honolulu and Australia. During an eleven-hour flight to Los Angeles one of the discs in Susan's lumbar region finally ruptured.

I'd never even thought about how uncomfortable the flight was going to be when I booked the holiday. I'd always managed on holidays in the past.

But about a month before the holiday the pain was getting worse and worse. I was so fed up because I'd spent lots of money on all these treatments that I saw my doctor and demanded that something was done. I was again referred to another rheumatologist, who in turn referred me for physiotherapy. The physiotherapy I received about a week before going on holiday was very vigorous. I lay on the floor on my back and the physiotherapist pulled my legs up and down.

Four hours into the first of their holiday flights, Susan, who was sitting at a window seat, struggled past a passenger to go to the loo.

Doing that felt a bit uncomfortable and by the time I got to the toilet I was in such agony I was too scared to sit down. I called a stewardess to help me. As it turned out my disc had finally ruptured.

It was a terrible start to the holiday. I was in absolute agony and had to lie across a few seats at the back of the plane with seven hours to go before touch-down at Los Angeles. It was a nightmare. I took painkillers to help relieve the pain and was given ice in a bag which melted all over my clothes which then had to be taken off me. When we arrived at the airport I had to be taken to hospital by ambulance.

In hospital I had such an enormous pain-killing injection I passed out. I had an x-ray and was told I had a problem with a disc. Even so we decided to carry on with our holiday – it was supposed to be the holiday of a lifetime after all and I was determined not to go home. I had three days' bed-rest in Los Angeles, then managed to get on the plane to go to Honolulu where I spent a week in bed. It was a good job there was a minibar in the hotel room and at least the weather was bad! I felt more for my husband. What a holiday of a lifetime.

Susan was treated by a chiropractor during this time and was prescribed herbal muscle relaxants which eased her discomfort. She and her husband carried on with their holiday in Australia and by the end Susan's back was slightly better. But the flight home was another story.

It was terrible. I was in such pain one of the stewards got me into First Class where I was able to lie on a recliner and so fell asleep. As soon as I got home I let rip at my doctor. He immediately referred me to a surgeon. I got a private consultation because there was no way I could go on a waiting list.

Susan was anxious about surgery but did have faith in the operation, particularly in view of the new techniques used.

Yes, I was frightened, but that was mainly because of the things other people kept telling me, like what if I ended up in a wheelchair. But I didn't even have to have a myelogram (see page 60) – a special kind of x-ray technique which can show up the bulge of a prolapsed disc – I had a body scan instead. The operation was so successful that when I woke up from surgery I thought they hadn't done it. I felt only slight discomfort. When nurses offered me pain relief all I needed was a couple of paracetamol! I was left with a tiny scar, it's only about an inch and a half long, and I was in hospital for about five days.

FIBROSITIS

Fibrositis – inflammation of white fibrous tissue, especially that of muscle sheaths – is a term sometimes used to describe pain due to stiffness in the muscles rather than to the bony changes that occur in the various forms of arthritis. Sometimes people feel the pain of fibrositis without any obvious record of injury and it often appears in the shoulders and neck. Usually, sufferers may be able to point to one spot where the pain will be when they press it, pain similar to that which they feel at other times – when they move their shoulder, for example. It's likely that these hot spots are sites of inflammation. This means that if they could be viewed directly they would be locally swollen, would be red because of the opening up of the small blood vessels as nature tries to heal the hurt, and hotter than usual to the touch.

Fibrositis is usually caused by tension and bad posture and middle-aged, elderly and anxious people suffer particularly. Attacks are often worse in the winter and exposure to cold and draughts may be a cause. Hot baths, massage and exercises to relax the tense muscles will usually relieve the pain, along with taking painkillers.

Although fibrositis may be regarded as a common but harmless complaint, after suffering a week of pain because of the condition a few years ago, Veronica, a sixty-three-year-old housewife, takes care not to risk developing it again. 'I'm quite sure I know what triggered it,' she says. 'I was out delivering leaflets when I got caught in the rain. I put on a mac a little later on top of my damp and cold cotton dress. The very next day I noticed twinges of pain right across the back of my shoulders.'

Initially, Veronica's shoulders weren't too uncomfortable, but within a couple of days the pain was enough to disturb her sleep.

> I couldn't even sit up straight or bend forward without being in a lot of pain. I couldn't pick up things from the floor or carry any shopping. It was awful.
>
> I had to sit leaning backwards with my shoulders propped on pillows or cushions before I could get any ease. Moving around or walking seemed to help

as well. Sitting still actually seemed to make it worse.

When Veronica saw her doctor he told her she had fibrositis, which could well have been triggered by her getting cold and damp.

Being told what was wrong put my mind at rest; I was beginning to imagine all sorts of things, that I was developing arthritis or something. The doctor also gave me Nurofen tablets which worked very well and meant that I had an uninterrupted night's sleep, as well as a cream containing a local anaesthetic called Transvasin.

Massaging my shoulders with this cream was a definite help. Either my husband or one of my daughters would rub it in for me and it was extremely relaxing.

Although I haven't had fibrositis like that since then, I have noticed that if the weather is damp I do find that I have rheumatic pains in my legs as well as my shoulders.

I do take care not to develop fibrositis again if I can help it. I always sit with a cardigan over my shoulders, a cotton one even in summer. If I can I avoid sitting in draughts and I definitely avoid getting caught in the rain without a mac.

OSTEOPOROSIS

Of course, the older you get, the more likely you are to experience back pain because joints and muscles do lose their elasticity. But back problems in older people aren't always caused by the ageing process and the loss of suppleness. Osteoporosis, a thinning of the bones, is a painful condition that can cause crippling back problems and can lead to unbelievably painful fractures in the spine, as vertebrae can crumble without any cause if they are badly weakened by osteoporosis. Some sufferers have several fractures which are terribly painful – both when they happen and as they heal, which can take many months. These back fractures can also change a sufferer's shape, making the back bent and causing several inches of height loss.

In osteoporosis, bones become brittle and cannot withstand the wear and tear of everyday activities and so break easily. Indeed, sufferers who fracture a hip often believe a fall has caused it when, in fact, it's more likely that the weight of the body alone was enough to bring about the fracture, which then caused them to trip and stumble.

Back pain can be an early symptom of osteoporosis. Often one or more of the vertebrae, especially those in the neck, can crumble slightly, resulting in pressure and pain, and can also trap nerves which causes more pain. In badly affected sufferers, osteoporosis of the spinal bones alone, without any fractures, can reduce height by up to ten inches. In many cases the upper spine curves, which in turn causes back pain and height loss. This curving of the spine is known as Dowager's Hump and shouldn't be considered the inevitable sign of getting old as it so often is.

Women after the menopause are particularly prone to thinning of the bones – as many as one in four women following the menopause is likely to develop osteoporosis compared with less than one in forty men of that age. Men have a denser bone structure than women which makes them less at risk, but it also may be because they don't have the dramatic reduction of the hormone oestrogen that women undergo during the menopause. This hormone is particularly important in cases of osteoporosis because it helps the body to absorb the calcium it needs for the maintenance of strong, healthy bones. At the same time women produce more of the male hormone, testosterone, so their ratio of testosterone to oestrogen rises.

As men get older their bodies stop making so much testosterone, but still produce a small amount of the female hormone oestrogen. So, in later years, for them it is the ratio of oestrogen to testosterone that increases. But things aren't as straightforward as they at first may seem. Research is beginning to imply that giving testosterone to a male osteoporosis sufferer may help, so the oestrogen/testosterone balance is not as clear cut as originally thought.

But one thing is certain, if you're a woman the older you are the more likely you are to be affected by osteoporosis. Half of women over the age of seventy-five will develop osteoporosis. Small, fair, thin-boned women are particularly at risk, and unfortunately it does run in families because mothers and sisters are likely to be of similar build. Also prolonged use of some drugs such as steroids, anti-convulsants and antacids can lead to osteoporosis. Other factors that make it more likely include a late puberty or an early menopause, not having children, illnesses such as rheumatoid arthritis, hyperparathyroidism – when the thyroid gland overproduces its hormone, Calcitonin – and asthma. Excessive smoking or drinking and not enough regular exercise can also be contributory.

Osteoporosis has been referred to as 'the silent epidemic'. Silent because it develops without being noticed, until, that is, the person breaks or fractures a bone. Yet most osteoporosis is now thought to be preventable and the sad thing is that those women suffering back and other mobility problems because of osteoporosis might have been able to avoid developing the disease in the first place.

If you're thinking of prevention, you need to be planning ten to twenty years ahead at least. Developing strong, healthy bones and so preventing osteoporosis depends partly on maintaining a good supply of the mineral calcium in our diet. This is particularly important during childhood, adolescence, pregnancy and while breastfeeding, and also the ten years before the menopause and for ten years after, when the body's absorption of calcium becomes less effi-cient due to hormonal changes.

Opinions vary on the merits of a high-calcium diet in later life, but most experts are in agreement that a diet lacking in sufficient quantities of calcium in early and middle life makes osteoporosis more likely. A good, calcium-rich diet should contain at least three servings a day of milk group food (some people believe four servings for the over sixties), for example, a glass of milk, a carton of yogurt and two ounces of cheese. Nuts, tinned salmon and sardines eaten with their bones, many dark green, leafy vegetables such as kale, spinach and broccoli are good for your bones. But vitamin D, which comes from sunshine as well as good food, is also important as we need it to ensure the calcium in our diet is absorbed. No wonder we were all encouraged as children to drink up our milk, eat our greens and then run around outside at school playtimes. It really wasn't just to give our teachers some peace and quiet!

Usually there continues to be a build-up of bone density until about the age of thirty-five, when the renewal process slows down and gradual loss of bone mass starts to occur. Bone density can now be measured and there are screening centres to which your doctor can refer you to help pinpoint those people at risk from the disease. There are different types of bone-density scans as well as x-rays available to try to diagnose the problem accurately. There is also the possibility of blood and urine samples being examined to find out whether you are short of oestrogen or whether you may be losing calcium.

Interestingly, according to the Arthritis and Rheumatism Council for Research, studies in Belgium have found that people with osteoarthritis in many joints are less likely to develop osteoporosis. In osteoarthritis bone mass increases which may mean that you are less at risk of osteoporosis. Also, osteoporosis is one of the few conditions that is actually likely to be less severe in overweight women. It seems fat stores may act as an oestrogen-producing organ and the extra oestrogen protects the woman from bone-thinning. In addition, the extra weight a heavy woman has to carry puts more stress upon the bones and this also helps to prevent thinning.

Vigorous weight-bearing exercise – brisk walking or

tennis, for example – has the same effect. Bone is a living tissue and using a limb definitely encourages the bones to grow, providing the constant push and pull on them that helps to keep them strong. Research has shown that you need walk only a few miles a week to cut down bone loss. When a person remains inactive for a long time they can quickly lose calcium from their bones and even the fittest can develop some degree of osteoporosis. That's why back problems can suddenly develop following a long, enforced stay in bed or after being wheelchair-bound. Pain can emerge as a result of bone compression in the spine after thinning.

But don't be misled into thinking that you need to be ill and immobile for your bones to become less than healthy. If you're an office worker, spending long hours at your desk, with the drive to and from work your only form of exercise, you're at risk of developing osteoporosis too.

There is a great deal of debate about the best methods of treatment. Calcium supplements should only be needed if your diet fails to provide you with enough. Treatments suggested have included calcium and fluoride tablets, calcitonin injections (to maintain bone density), painkillers, chemicals called biphosphonates, anabolic steroids or other newly developed medicines as well as physiotherapy and hydrotherapy in some cases.

But in my opinion, for most women, hormone replacement therapy (HRT), begun at the time of the menopause and continued for at least ten years, is the most effective way to prevent osteoporosis. HRT provides the means of administering the female hormone oestrogen – levels of which, as I've said, drop dramatically after the menopause.

So topping up oestrogen levels helps stop bone loss as well as menopausal symptoms such as hot flushes and sweats. Initially, there were worries about HRT increasing risks of womb cancer but these days, to lessen this risk, a combination of oestrogen and the other female hormone progesterone is usually prescribed.

Most doctors now agree on the benefits of hormone

replacement therapy and, whether or not a female sufferer is having menopausal symptoms, many doctors will still prescribe it.

One disadvantage of HRT is that most women will have menstrual periods and even monthly breast tenderness. But the advantages are stronger bones and muscles, better looking skin, the continuity of normal vaginal secretions, no hot flushes and a reduced risk of heart disease.

Studies show that both heart disease and female cancers of the uterus and ovaries are less frequent in women taking HRT. Because many, if not most, cancers of the breast can be treated by stopping a woman's body from producing oestrogen, or blocking its action, it has been suggested that HRT, which relies on oestrogen, could be a 'cause' of breast cancer. The expert researchers continue to debate the subject but the evidence has not been seen to be sufficient to alter the recommendation for HRT in a fit woman – the advantages appear to heavily outweigh any potential disadvantages. And since the problems with side-effects from HRT are few for most women, I would have no qualms in taking it if I were a healthy woman.

The worrying thing about back problems caused by osteoporosis is that the disease is on the increase. According to the National Osteoporosis Society, at the end of the 1960s there were 10,000 hip fractures a year; now there are more than 45,000, costing the NHS more than £200 million per annum. The disease causes pain and fractures in more than two million women in the UK and more women die from osteoporosis-related fractures than from cancer of the ovaries, cervix and uterus combined. One in five women who suffer a hip fracture dies not long afterwards.

Almost six years ago, Barbara, then a fifty-seven-year-old housewife, tripped down the altar steps at church which resulted in a crush fracture in her lower spine. At that time she just thought the fracture would heal in due course and that that would be the end of the pain in her back. She had no idea that the fracture was a result of osteoporosis and that it would soon change her life quite drastically.

When I tripped I knew I'd done something serious because I heard a short, sharp crack. I was told by my doctor to go to bed and rest for a couple of weeks. But I was in horrendous pain with very bad muscle spasm as well. I had a board under my mattress. I slept in a double bed on my own which meant I could move about more easily and slowly to get comfortable. That helped tremendously.

Six months later, Barbara couldn't walk very easily and was in a lot of pain.

If I lay still I was OK. Moving was painful and I had to take painkillers every four hours. I couldn't do housework or shopping. My husband had to do most things. I'd always been an active person and all this made me feel very frustrated, especially when my Mini was sold because it was too difficult for me to get down into such a small car and then drive.

Nine months later Barbara was still in pain and changed her doctor. She was finally tested for osteoporosis. The subsequent confirmation of the condition was followed by light physiotherapy.

And general exercises to get my legs going again so that I could walk. I was then referred to an osteoporosis consultant. She explained the problem to me in detail. I was also told that if I didn't start taking calcium and vitamin D as well as HRT I'd be confined to a wheelchair in ten years time.

Once I'd been told all the facts I felt much better. I've found that HRT has been tremendously helpful. In two years my bone density has increased from 60 per cent to 77 per cent.

In other words, it can be seen on an x-ray film that her bones have hardened from 60 per cent of their pre-osteoporosis strength, to 77 per cent after she'd been taking the HRT.

Unfortunately, Barbara had another fall down her front door steps a few months ago. The result was another spinal fracture.

> I fell awkwardly and also hurt my ribs and arm. I now have a GP I have complete confidence in who has told me that he didn't know that much about osteoporosis but that he would make it his business to find out as much as he could. With this fracture I've been much happier with the treatment I've received.
>
> I was given valium as a temporary measure to control the painful muscle spasms in my back. Three months later I'm up and walking about and wearing a corset and I have less pain than I did with the last fracture.

Barbara has had a history of breast lumps and since osteoporosis was diagnosed she has had to have a mastectomy because of breast cancer. She also had to stop taking HRT because she had an oestrogen-dependant tumour. As I mentioned earlier, once a breast cancer shows up the success of the treatment will be enhanced if the patient stops taking oestrogen by mouth and her own body's natural oestrogen production is blocked – prevented from having many of its normal actions within her body. This is often achieved nowadays by Tamoxifen, a medicine taken by mouth. Many specialists will allow a woman to take HRT again if, after two years, no further signs of the cancer can be found.

So now Barbara is taking other measures to protect her bones.

> I'm careful about my diet. I eat plenty of cheese, drinks lots of milk. I take calcium and vitamin D tablets. My problem is walking up and down stairs

which is very difficult. As for exercise I've started walking. I can't walk very far. I try to walk up and down the road every day because exercise is so important for me to try to stop my bones deteriorating. And my husband also pushes me in a wheelchair for long walks as it's important to get fresh air and sunshine.

I've found that osteoporosis is a very painful condition and you have to learn to live with it. I've been counselled for cancer and I think the positive thinking you need to adopt to fight cancer is the same attribute you need to fight osteoporosis.

I'm small boned and fair but I've had plenty of exercise in my life and I've always eaten well. In the early eighties I used to diet a lot because I was always afraid of putting on weight. With hindsight I wonder whether that was a good thing. I did have small amounts of cheese and milk then. Nobody seemed to warn you about the dangers of osteoporosis in those days. And I think women really should be made more aware of it. Osteoporosis isn't an inevitable part of the menopause or something women should have to put up with.

ARTHRITIS

Various forms of arthritis also commonly cause back pain.

Osteoarthritis, or degenerative joint disease, is the most common form of arthritis – there are probably five million sufferers in this country alone – and can often affect the joints of the spine. Although it's referred to as the wear-and-tear type of arthritis, over-use of joints doesn't *cause* arthritis, but does seem to play a part in how badly you develop the disease. That's probably why osteoarthritis is so common among older people. X-rays of people's backs show that osteoarthritis affects nearly everyone over fifty and this may result in pain.

Back pain can be quite a problem in cases of osteoarthritis because it damages joint surfaces, inhibiting the painless and proper use of a joint – and with so many joints to choose from in the back you can see why it can cause so much trouble.

When osteoarthritis develops, the protective, shock-absorbing rubbery substance called cartilage, which covers the ends of the bones to protect them, becomes worn and rough and almost 'rubbed away'. In places it splits so that the bone underneath thickens and spreads out, enlarging the joint. The bones rub against each other, and the pain may seem particularly bad after keeping still. Bony outgrowths or spurs – known as osteophytes – may develop at the edges of the joints. When this happens on the vertebrae it can press on the nerves causing pain or, at worse, paralysis of the muscles that the nerve 'controls'.

Osteoarthritis can be an extremely painful condition which tends to involve a gradual deterioration and a slow onset of pain and disfigurement. Osteoarthritis mainly affects the hips, knees and fingers as well as the spine. Sometimes the neck and lower back are affected.

The individual vertebrae, as well as the joints and discs between each, and their associated ligaments, can all show such wear and tear in x-rays. The spine at the top (in the neck) is particularly prone to this condition; it's then called cervical spondylosis. If it's in the lower back, it's called lumbar spondylosis. The symptoms caused will often be due to the pressure on the nerves as they leave the nervous system through the spaces between each of the vertebra. These gradually become narrowed as part of the wear and tear process, and the pressure on the nerves can cause pain, numbness or changed sensations.

'Spondylosis' literally means 'inflammation of the spine' but here it's used to describe the condition when the joints between the vertebrae don't move as easily, one upon another, as they did before. This can be because they form fibre and bony attachments between them. It is also loosely used to mean the degenerative changes which are seen in osteoarthritis.

Scott, a sixty-three-year-old retired plumber, has known the crippling effects of osteoarthritis. He's suffered with back pain for more than twenty-five years because of it.

> I had a back injury at work more than thirty years ago when I was bending a copper pipe across my knee. I twisted my spine, damaged a nerve and two discs prolapsed.
>
> I was told at hospital that I would probably have arthritis in my spine later in life because of the injury. But I seemed to develop it about five years afterwards.
>
> I noticed pain in the lumbar region and down my left leg. I had a nagging pain all the time which was worse when I lifted heavy weights, or when I was bending down at work.
>
> I've seen many doctors in my time and been given all sorts of painkillers like co-proxamol and ibuprofen, rubs and sprays. I've had physiotherapy and manipulation, heat treatment both privately and on the NHS. I've found that warmth helps, even by keeping my body warm during the day by wearing a vest and a few layers of clothes in the winter.

During Scott's forties the pain and stiffness began to get much worse. His sleep became more disturbed which meant he felt irritable the next day and also more aware of his back pain because he felt so tired.

> In bed at night my back would become very painful. I'd have to keep moving about all night long trying to find a comfortable position. I've tried all manner of things to make me comfortable, from buying a harder mattress, putting a board under the bed, and rolling a scarf tightly to form a sausage-like pillow to support the small of my back. Nothing cures the

pain, although some things give you momentary ease. To be honest the greatest relief I get is sitting in a warm bath, but once I get out of the bath the pain returns soon afterwards.

It's now progressively getting worse. Bending is becoming very difficult. If I get down on my knees to play with my young grandson I find it's very difficult to get up again. Walking up stairs is difficult but it's even more painful to walk down steps or stairs. If I drop something I feel like a rusty mechanical man when I try to pick it up again. But being in one position for too long irritates my back.

Walking is getting more difficult when the back pain is troubling me. The pain in my back is like having severe toothache along the length of the lower part of the spine and across the bottom of my back. Cold and damp weather seem to make it worse.

I find it's important to keep moving and to be careful about how I sit. An upright hard chair is best – even then I can't sit too long in one position, I have to move.

At times in my life it's been hard going, especially trying to work as a plumber with so much bending and twisting. In the end I was forced to retire early at the age of fifty-eight when my back pain was becoming so bad that work was becoming unbearable and totally impractical.

Since then I try to carry on with my life as normal by taking painkillers when the pain gets too bad. I refuse to stop doing the things I want to do. I'm sure if I stopped my back would seize up so despite the pain I keep going by mainly using sprays and rubs to ease the pain as well as being determined not to let my back problems dominate my life.

Osteoarthritis sufferers aren't the only ones to be plagued with back problems, rheumatoid arthritis is another form of arthritis that can cause back trouble. Unlilke osteoarthritis, where it is usually the large weight-bearing joints which are affected, rheumatoid arthritis tends to strike the smaller joints in the hands, feet and wrists, for example. It can, however, progress further and develop in larger joints such as the knees, ankles, elbows, shoulders and hips, as well as causing inflammation and pain in the back. It's not as common as osteoarthritis – there are around half a million sufferers.

Just as in so many forms of arthritis, rheumatoid arthritis varies considerably from person to person. Basically, in disease, inflammation most often serves a useful purpose: protection. This isn't the case with the inflammation of rheumatoid arthritis, when somehow the protective process is 'reversed' – the inflammation itself causes damage, and it goes on damaging.

The swelling that follows is as a result both of a thickening of the synovial membrane which encases the joint and of the over-production of its usual lubricating fluid. Fluid and cells seep out of the inflamed membrane, disintegrating cartilage, which in turn forms erosions on the bones. So the whole joint, including muscle and tendons nearby, can become damaged. Rheumatoid arthritis doesn't usually affect the spine until the disease has been active for some time and then it's usually the neck that's affected.

Another form of arthritis involving the back is ankylosing spondylitis, a painful inflammation of the joints between the vertebrae so that the spinal column gradually becomes hard and inflexible. Joints of the back and hips are the main ones involved, but in a few cases shoulders, knees and ankles can be affected.

Interestingly, ankylosing spondylitis is considered to be one of the few rheumatic diseases that is more common in men and is nearly always thought of as a young man's disease. However, as we shall see, specialists now believe that because of misdiagnosis ankylosing spondylitis is often missed in women.

Rather than being a straightforward mechanical back

problem, ankylosing spondylitis is an inflammatory type of arthritis affecting just over one in a hundred people. 'Ankylosing' means stiffening and, as we have seen, 'spondylitis' inflammation of the spine. It starts insidiously over a period of weeks, usually at around the age of twenty to twenty-five. The pain stems from the sacroiliac joints – the joints, one on each side, which attach the spine to the pelvis. It's accompanied by stiffness and is felt normally in the lower back or perhaps as an ache in the buttocks. It tends to be worse in the early morning, after a night's rest, and for many sufferers seems to improve with stretching exercises or just walking around – although for some this alone can require determination.

Inflammation begins at the edges of the joints between the vertebrae. When the inflammation dies down, bone grows from both sides of the joint as part of the healing process. But eventually the bone can surround the joint completely, making it rigid. Unlike the sudden back pain of a slipped disc or pulled muscle, the pain and stiffness of ankylosing spondylitis is gradual and persistent, often described as 'creeping'. The bouts come and go, very often creeping up the spine. Although the pain usually affects the back, some sufferers have chest pains which are more severe when they breathe deeply. The pain stems from the joints between the ribs and the vertebrae.

The cause of ankylosing spondylitis is not known. It can run in families and it is now accepted that it is about three hundred times more common in people who have a white cell blood group known as MLA B27. These cells contain a protein – called a marker – which may be involved in the cause of the condition or the symptoms it brings on. Only about one in ten of the population inherit this group, and only two out of ten people with this particular white blood cell group will get ankylosing spondylitis.

If you suffer from ankylosing spondylitis then you should discuss the possibility of suddenly developing an inflammation of the eye called iritis or uveitis – inflammation of the iris and its surrounding tissues – which needs immediate treatment to prevent any permanent damage. If you experience blurred vision, especially with pain, and if your eye is bloodshot seek medical help immediately. It's thought that approximately four out of ten sufferers have experienced this at some time, and some specialists believe that sufferers should have eye-drops on hand at all times in their refrigerators in case of an attack.

It's important to get medical treatment early on if you have ankylosing spondylitis. One of the primary objectives is to avoid the sufferer's spine becoming set in a bent position – the worst disability following this disease. As well as an x-ray you may be tested for anaemia and also a blood test called the erythrocyte sedimentation rate (ESR) may be carried out to establish how active the disease is. The amount of damage done obviously depends on the severity of your symptoms. The main treatment is exercise and anti-inflammatory drugs to help get rid of pain and stiffness. Physiotherapy also plays a very important role and NASS, the National Ankylosing Spondylitis Society, has produced a twenty-minute cassette of physiotherapy exercises for those unable to get supervision (for their address, see page 101). In severe cases surgery has been recommended to straighten the spine – although this is now rare. Hip replacement surgery can be beneficial if the hip joints are badly damaged.

According to NASS, you should learn this motto like a catechism: It's the doctor's job to relieve the pain and the patient's job to keep exercising and to maintain a good posture. Sufferers find that no matter how much it hurts at the time, exercise really is beneficial, so keep mobile and stop joints sticking.

A common danger with a back problem like ankylosing spondylitis is misdiagnosis. NASS figures suggest that, for every sufferer, there has been an average of eight years misdiagnosis. As well as general lack of awareness of the problem, another difficulty is that no two cases are the same. Misdiagnosis occurs because there is no simple blood test to confirm the disease's presence – as in the case of the rheumatic disease lupus, for example – and x-rays don't always show up the damage for several years.

Exercise, as I've said, is very important, as thirty-three-year-old Peter, a petrol station manager and former butcher, has found to his relief. He'd suffered with back problems for almost seven years before ankylosing spondylitis was diagnosed early last year.

> I don't know how many doctors told me that they didn't know what was wrong with me. At one stage I even saw a neurologist. I think people were even trying to suggest that my symptoms were psychosomatic but I can assure you they weren't.
>
> It's just that initially I had this terrible tired feeling in my legs with pains at the top of my pelvis. Even when I'd been asleep all night my legs would still ache and feel tired in the morning – tired is the only way I can describe the sensation. I'd have a gnawing, toothache-like pain in them which would be relieved, strangely enough, by walking. It was originally put down to torn ligaments in the sacro-iliac joints.

Peter suffered this intense discomfort for two years before trying to find a solution through private medical treatment, visiting an orthopaedic surgeon in addition to a physiotherapist, but no one was able to pinpoint the problem exactly.

> I went privately because I was desperate to find out what was wrong with me. Although nobody seemed to know what it was, I was certain that it wasn't all in my mind.
>
> Physiotherapy did ease the symptoms. It made it bearable enough for me to get on with my life, supplemented by anti-inflammatory medicines. I tried chiropractic which didn't help and to be honest it seemed to make things worse.

By now Peter's pain spread to his lower back, which made walking extremely difficult.

> Up until this point I'd always managed to carry on working but now I had to take time off for the first time. The pain was in the lower area of my spine. It was excruciating. I couldn't sleep, couldn't walk, I couldn't get comfortable in any position even sitting or lying down.
>
> It was so depressing to find that after six years or so the problem was getting worse not better. And I still didn't really know what was causing it.

Finally Peter went back to a GP who suggested he had more investigations including a CT scan (computerised-axial tomography, see page 60) which showed he had torn ligaments in the sacroiliac joints, and an MRI (magnetic resonance image, see page 60) which seemed to suggest he had a ruptured disc.

> I also saw an osteopath who, while thinking I had torn ligaments, also thought I had another underlying problem and did in the end suggest I get a second opinion.
>
> The pain in my back was now becoming worse. I began to move about very slowly and my mobility got worse. Everyone looking at me could see how slow I was – although it all happened gradually I didn't realise just how slow I'd become.
>
> In all I must have spent at least £2000 trying to find out what was wrong with me. I do feel slightly bitter about it. I have two young children and the money would have been much better spent on them. But what good is money if you haven't got good health to enjoy it – that's why we kept paying to try to find a cure.
>
> I was referred privately to an orthopaedic surgeon. I had more x-rays and that was when

ankylosing spondylitis was finally diagnosed and I was surprised to learn that I now had to see a rheumatologist. I'd never even heard of the condition and had no idea it was a form of arthritis. All I cared about was the relief I felt when at last someone said, 'Yes, I really think I know what's wrong with you.'

By this time Peter had become round-shouldered and was stooping slightly. Within five days of seeing a rheumatologist he was in hospital for two weeks of physiotherapy, which mainly involved stretching exercises and hydrotherapy.

'I felt so positive about getting the right treatment at last,' he recalls. As I've mentioned, getting the correct treatment early on is important in ankylosing spondylitis. The amount of damage done does depend on how long and how badly you have the disease. For many people the disease causes few if any long-term problems; they have some pain and discomfort but lead normal active lives. In a very few these days the spine or other joints become bent or stuck and for them life can be very tough. If the disease is diagnosed and treated early this can often be prevented.

Peter believes that he was fortunate in finally discovering what was wrong with him so that he could take steps to prevent his condition deteriorating.

Finally finding out about ankylosing spondylitis did ease my mind but at the same time I wondered what the future held for me. But I now know that I have to manage my back problem myself. I'm taking anti-inflammatory tablets which help. Some days the pain is negligible although on others it can be bad.

Peter has found talking to other sufferers through meetings of NASS beneficial, as has been his own exercise programme.

I do stretching exercises at least six days a week for an hour. This definitely stops me seizing up and also strengthens my back muscles. I know that some people don't have the fight in them to beat the disease. You have to push yourself and manage the disease yourself. The medical profession can help you but believe me you have to help yourself.

RARER CAUSES OF BACK PROBLEMS

There are other rarer causes of back problems, such as a fractured spine which is potentially very serious because the spinal cord could be injured as a result of the fracture itself or as a result of the accident victim being inadvisedly moved. Arachnoiditis is a rare inflammation of the inner lining or dural sheath within the spinal canal. An infection, sometimes a bacterial infection, can cause an abscess in or near a vertebra. Very occasionally there may be an infection, called discitis, in the disc sometimes after treatment with chymopapain (chemonucleolysis, see page 61) to treat disc prolapse.

There always seems to be one letter in my postbag every now and then asking me whether back pain is a sign of cancer. It rarely is. Likewise, back pain is something thought, by the female sufferer, to be due to problems with her womb – fibroids, for example. Again, the problem is usually in the back itself. The cancers that occur in bone and that cause low back pain are almost always as a result of cancer elsewhere in the body.

Osteomalacia is a rare softening of the bones in adults because of a vitamin D deficiency, and, as we know, vitamin D is necessary for the absorption of calcium. It's the adult version of rickets if you like.

Paget's disease is a rare bone disease that causes the outer layer of bone to become thickened, resulting in severe deformities. It's more common in men, especially older men, and it mainly affects the bones of the spine, particularly the weight-bearing lumbosacral area, pelvis and legs, but also the skull. Pain – a dull and aching back and leg pain – is as a result of the bone deformities. Some sufferers even describe it as a gnawing type of pain, especially at night when they're in bed. Not all sufferers, however, experience pain, especially when the disease is in an advanced state, as then they're only aware of a deformity in their bones. Sometimes symptoms may initially arise as pain in the hip, thigh or arm.

Current research suggests that in genetically susceptible people viruses contracted earlier in life could play a part in Paget's disease – viruses such as measles or the respiratory syncytial virus which causes a 'flu-like' illness. With advances in treatment and new drugs, it's thought that the gross deformities caused by the disease could very soon become a thing of the past.

PREGNANCY AND LOOKING AFTER YOUNG CHILDREN

In some cases back pain is caused by conditions which have nothing to do with the back at all, such as pregnancy. As many as one in six pregnant women complain of some degree of back pain, in fact it can be so common in pregnancy that some women take it for granted! From the early months of pregnancy, until about six months after the birth, you may be more likely to suffer backache.

Dawn, a thirty-two-year-old designer, first had an incident of back pain when she was twenty-six. The pain was so severe she was unable to work for three days and even slept on the floor to ease it.

> I must have lifted something badly although I'm not sure what caused the pain. There wasn't one particular incident that triggered it. What I do know is that it was extremely painful, especially when I tried to stand, and moving was also very difficult. The pain was in the middle of my back towards the lower region. I don't know whether I had a ropey

old bed at the time and that had something to do with it. I found that sleeping on the floor helped, as did having a piece of chipboard under my mattress – which I still have.

Since that time Dawn has had two children and with both pregnancies the back problem resurfaced during the fourth to seventh month. Again, the pain wasn't triggered by one particular incident, but would appear when Dawn had been overdoing things.

If I did too much ironing, or gardening, or lifting my oldest child, or walking, or anything physical really, I'd have an aching, continuous pain in the middle to lower back area once more. It wasn't a throbbing pain, more of a pain that stops you getting comfortable in any one position.

I found various ways of dealing with it, though. I tried to sit on a low stool about six or seven inches off the ground. This meant that when I sat I was almost squatting and I could lean forward slightly. I found this very helpful because it seemed to take away any pressure from my lower back. I'm sure you hold yourself differently during pregnancy and your increased weight and changed shape tend to swing you forward which I suppose must put more pressure on your back.

Yoga was another thing that I found really helpful. During both pregnancies I went to active yoga classes every week for five months, from the time I was four months' pregnant until just before I gave birth. As well as learning to breathe properly in order to relax, and stand properly, the positions involved lots of gentle stretching movements which I found very helpful for my back.

Massage was another element of the classes and this definitely helped ease the pain. We would get on our knees with knees apart and lean forward on

our elbows so it stretched out our backs, and then
we would take turns to massage each other's backs.
This position itself was useful and the massage was
very soothing.

It can be difficult to establish exactly what gives rise to
back pain in pregnancy as there are a number of possible
causes. During pregnancy the ligaments that surround all
the joints in the body become softened so they have more
give in them, thus putting increased pressure on nerves and
muscles. This happens early on when the two hormones,
progesterone and relaxin, are produced in increased
amounts. By thirty-eight weeks the ligaments are at their
most stretchy in readiness for the birth. Women who
already have one child can find that their ligaments are even
more loose with a subsequent pregnancy.

The shape of the spinal column alters and the pelvic joints
expand, so any underlying imbalance in the mechanics of
the spine will be affected during pregnancy. There is also a
shift in your centre of gravity as you get bigger. Some
women find that their waist has grown by as much as
twenty inches and that it is nigh on impossible to lean back
from the waist to counter-balance this weight. Abdominal
muscles also stretch to cope with this excess baggage and
that can pull on the spine.

Another cause of back pain in pregnancy can be strain in
the sacroiliac joints (the joints between the sacrum and the
pelvic bones). The ligaments around these joints relax
towards the end of pregnancy, but this means they and the
other joints in the back are more easily strained for up to six
months after childbirth. To help avoid strain you should be
careful about how you get into and out of bed – don't heave
yourself up with a big jerk but roll on to your side, keep your
knees together when you put your feet on the floor and
push your body up by using your arms.

Pain caused by tension in the muscles surrounding and
supporting the spine is common. It is often felt as back pain
or, if muscle tension is on the front of the spine, as

abdominal pain. Tension in the back muscles high in the neck may pull on the skull. Some women even find that the weight of enlarged breasts can cause discomfort between the shoulder blades.

It's not that uncommon for a pregnant woman to suffer sciatica if the baby lies against the sciatic nerve, as I mentioned on pages 11–12. Some women also complain of back pain following an epidural – an injection that is given into the sheath surrounding the central nervous system and which lies within the spinal column. This anaesthetises the nerves so that, for example, an operation on the lower part of the body can be undertaken without pain and while the patient, or mother-to-be if it is being given during child-birth, is still awake. Though not common, some patients do complain of pain following an epidural injection, but this should decrease with time.

Always take medical advice on back pain in pregnancy to rule out any underlying condition. And follow basic rules for avoiding back pain generally. For example, don't wear high heels – the higher the heels the more likely they are to put a strain on your back because of the unnatural position it's forced to adopt. Once the baby is born, if you like to carry him or her in a sling make sure it's positioned so that the baby's head is just under your chin otherwise your back muscles will have to counterbalance the weight. And don't stoop when you push your pram or buggy, try to stand keeping your shoulders in a natural position.

Remember you don't have to grin and bear painful backache in pregnancy or afterwards. Talk to your doctor as there may be an obstetric physiotherapist at your hospital who will be able to advise you and suggest some helpful exercises.

As parents quickly discover, looking after babies and toddlers can be pretty exhausting. It can also result in back problems for many people, if the letters in my postbag are anything to go by.

Putting babies and toddlers into and picking them up out of car seats can be one of the easiest ways for a parent to hurt his or her back, as Vivienne, a forty-year-old mother, discovered.

I found with my two children that the problem started when they reached the age of about nine months or so, when they become that bit heavier. The problem gets worse as they get older because they just get heavier and heavier.

Putting them into highchairs can be difficult. I found that it helped if I put them in from behind the chair rather than lifting them over the tray. But the worst thing of all for me was putting them into car seats. You find yourself in such an awkward position, leaning forward with your back extended and no support. It's almost impossible to get your weight underneath you.

When my first child was about fourteen months old and weighed about twenty-eight pounds I was trying to put him into the car seat and my back just went. I ended up in a huge heap on the pavement unable to move and about two miles from home – although the distance was irrelevant as I could have been just a hundred yards away, it wouldn't have made any difference, I couldn't move.

Meanwhile Alexis was climbing around inside the car trying to get out. I stopped a passerby and asked whether she would ring my next-door neighbour, which she kindly did. The passerby waited until she arrived and tried to keep Alexis in the car. I managed to sit on the ledge by the open car door and wedged myself into a semi-comfortable position while we waited. When my neighbour arrived she put Alexis into her car seat and I slowly crawled head-first into the back of her car.

Vivienne had in fact torn a muscle in her back and was in such pain she had to rest in bed for four days before things improved.

After that incident I tried to take the strain off my back by making sure the car seat was secured as close to the passenger door as possible, and I would hold the child across my arms instead of holding them under the arms then twisting my body to put them into the seat. I'd also bend my knees and rest them against the side of the passenger seat so that I'd be leaning forward slightly but supported at the same time.

As Vivienne's story clearly demonstrates, you have to think about how you lift a child, whether it's into a highchair, in and out of the bath, or strapping them into a car seat.

Michaela, a thirty-three-year-old mother, found that by the time her son was about twelve months old she had back pain virtually every day.

The aches and pains in my back started off very slowly but gradually became quite uncomfortable. I wouldn't have pain at the same spot either. Some days my shoulders and across the top of my ribs would ache. Other days my spine itself seemed to ache from about halfway down to the bottom. And on other days I could feel that the muscles, one each side of my lower back, were almost screaming, 'Enough is enough!'

By the end of the day the pain would be at its worst. But in the morning, after a night's rest, it would have either disappeared completely or would have gone by the following day. I soon realised that it was time I looked carefully at just what I was doing during the day. I was frightened that if I didn't take action my back would completely seize up and then I'd have real problems.

Michaela found lifting her son Owen into and out of his highchair put a strain on her back. During the day she decided to feed him while he was sitting on her lap, which meant she would only use the highchair at night when her husband was around.

> I decided I had to ask John to lift Owen as much as he could when he was at home in the evening.
>
> During the day I was also careful about how I picked Owen up. Once he could walk I would try not to pick him up so much. If we had to go upstairs I would hold his hands and help him walk up instead of carrying him. If I had to pick him up I made sure that I bent my knees and almost squatted before lifting him and holding him very close to my body. I do this every time I have to lift him and if I also have to put him in his pushchair I still try to keep my back straight and my knees bent with my feet quite far apart. I'm sure I must look very strange sometimes but I don't care.
>
> To change his nappy I either sit next to him on the bed, or change him while he lies across my lap, or I kneel on the floor – leaning over the bed or his changing table just added to the strain on my back.

Lifting children in and out of the bath is another common way of damaging your back. Michaela has found her own technique to prevent this:

> When I give Owen a bath I make sure I sit on a low stool at the side of the tub, then I lift him on to my lap before the bath. I also adjusted the height of the mattress in his cot. The mattress is now slightly higher so that I don't have to lower him so far down and again I try to keep my knees bent and pressed against the side of the cot when I put him in or lift him out. It seems to me that cots are really badly designed when it comes to looking after your back. It's so difficult to bend your knees and lean forward to lower a heavy baby on to the mattress.

All the things that I decided to do were simple measures really but within a week my back problems started to disappear. They do recur, though, if I'm lazy and don't think about my back throughout the day.

As Michaela points out, it's helpful to change your baby's nappy either on a changing mat placed at a height which saves you bending too far or placed on the floor so you can kneel down. If you do put your baby at a height that prevents you from stooping, do make sure you never leave the baby unattended, and don't turn your back even for a second – they can fall off from even the earliest age.

Finally, try to resist the temptation of balancing the baby on one hip while you stand. This can lead to quite bad back pain as your spine is forced to maintain almost a sideways curve which also puts a strain on muscles. It's less stressful for your back if you try to hold your child in the centre of your body with his or her legs around your waist – although with the wriggling toddlers I know that's sometimes easier said than done.

CONVENTIONAL TREATMENT

BED REST AND PAINKILLERS

While one and a half million people in this country are suffering some degree of back pain at any one time, the majority do actually get better on their own with no more than bed rest and/or painkilling drugs.

The treatment of back pain usually involves immobilisation, rest and the relief of pain. Busy people find that it's difficult to relax and many feel that resting in bed is not a 'proper' treatment, or even feel guilty that they are stuck in bed doing nothing. In fact bed rest is helpful. Most back pains are due to strains, sprains and tears and the injured part needs a period of rest while healing gets underway, followed by a further period of gentle exercise and rehabilitation.

Research has now shown, however, that staying in bed for *too long* could make the problem worse, because the muscles of the body quickly lose their tone – immediate strength – when they remain unexercised. The process can happen within a few days so that the sufferer feels very weak when he or she first gets out of bed. As I mentioned before, the muscles around the vertebrae work under the greatest mechanical difficulty, so if they lose their tone, the back is further disadvantaged, over and above the condition that caused the sufferer to take to his or her bed in the first place.

Some experts believe that sufferers should get up and start moving about as soon as the pain eases enough to be able to do so. Spending too much time in bed can also be bad for your circulation.

So, if you have to rest in bed try to move around gently from time to time, changing position or even just wriggling your toes; rotate your ankles in a clockwise direction then back again, and raise and lower your knees several times if you can.

Initial treatment for back trouble usually involves dealing with the pain. Basic mechanical back problems are likely to be dealt with by your GP who'll probably advise rest and will in all likelihood offer you tablets to relieve pain and/or inflammation.

Aspirin and other non-steroidal anti-inflammatory drugs like ibuprofen and naproxen or naprosyn, which can alleviate pain as well as reducing stiffness and inflammation, can be helpful. Aspirin can also be bought over the counter under brand marks or trade names such as Aspro or Solnin.

Remember, though, that aspirin is known to cause stomach irritation. That's why it shouldn't be taken on an empty stomach, at the very least with a glass of milk. Don't drink alcohol either when you're taking aspirin, it only adds to the likelihood of your stomach being irritated.

Aspirin or other anti-inflammatory and pain-relieving medicines like ibuprofen are the most useful over-the-counter medicines for the relief of back pain. There are again various brands on the market like Nurofen, Proflex or Inoven. These help to relax tenseness in the muscles which only adds to the pain you might be in.

Ibuprofen is a popular option when it comes to dealing with back pain. It's thought to work by blocking the enzyme needed for the production of prostaglandins, which would pass on pain signals to the brain. Prostaglandins also cause inflammation, heat and swelling which makes you feel even worse and can inhibit movement. It has been found to be effective in reducing pain and tenderness and one clinical trial has even suggested that it can help reduce the length of time that pain lasts. The trial involved sixty footballers with injuries ranging from trauma to joints or muscles, to sprained muscles or ligaments. Players given ibuprofen were able to get back to training sessions and achieve match fitness earlier than the control group treated with aspirin.

Ibuprofen shouldn't be used by people with stomach

ulcers or other stomach disorders. People sensitive to aspirin may also be sensitive to ibuprofen, yet it has been found to be gentler on the stomach than aspirin and as a result is as well tolerated as paracetemol.

Asthma sufferers and anyone who is allergic to aspirin should only take ibuprofen after consulting their doctor. It's not usually prescribed for pregnant women.

Indomethacin, another non-steroidal anti-inflammatory drug used in the treatment of arthritis, can sometimes be prescribed for back pain, as can muscle relaxants such as diazepam or methocarbamol (Robaxin or Robaxisal Forte).

Paracetamol, or combined analgesics – co-codamol, co-proxamol, co-dydramol – are often prescribed depending on the intensity of your pain, but bear in mind that whilst it may be an extremely effective painkiller it will not help reduce inflammation. (It can nevertheless be useful if you can't tolerate aspirin.) Like aspirin, paracetamol is widely available under own brand names or trade names such as Panadol or Paraclear. Other painkillers contain mixtures of paracetamol and codeine, such as Solpadeine, or paracetamol, aspirin and codeine in the case of Veganin, which might be useful in controlling rheumatic pain.

There are other products on the market specifically aimed at back pain, such as Doan's, which contains paracetamol and sodium salicylate, a mild pain reliever.

To be most effective, over-the-counter painkillers need to be taken at regular intervals, according to the instructions given on the packet. By taking these painkillers regularly a constant level of pain relief is maintained in the bloodstream and consequently pain is thwarted from resurfacing. But with any painkiller, don't take it for more than a few days, unless your doctor has told you otherwise. And whatever you do, don't mix and match painkillers. Always consult your doctor or pharmacist before taking an over-the-counter medicine if you are already taking medication or have a medical condition. Don't think that by taking a lot of painkillers in one go they'll work better, this is not the case. Never exceed the stated dose – overdoses can be dangerous.

If you're one of those people who are averse to taking tablets you'll be pleased to know that massaging the affected area of your back or the painful muscle can be soothing. You don't have to use a vibrator or a liniment or muscle rub although there are plenty on the market.

Your doctor may also prescribe one of the topical non-steroidal anti-inflammatory drugs like Feldene Gel, or Movelat or Traxam, which you apply to the affected area usually up to four times a day in most cases. These can be helpful in relieving pain and inflammation. But not all patients will be suitable for these preparations, particularly those suffering from asthma or those allergic to aspirin.

You may also be prescribed one of the many counter-irritants, like Algipan containing methyl nicotinate, which make the skin redden and therefore warm, so easing muscular pain and stiffness. Another possibility is a cream like Transvasin, containing benzocaine, a local anaesthetic.

Treatments available over the counter include Algipan Rub and Spray; Bengue's Balsam; Boots Warming Pain Relief Spray; Boots Icy-Gel Muscle Rub; Boots Pain Relieving Balm; the Deep Heat range of products; Massage Balm; Methol and Wintergreen Rub; PR Freeze Spray; PR Heat Spray; and the Radian-B range, among others; as well as herbal rubs like Dr Valnet's Flexarome, Gonne Balm, Natural Olbas Oil or Nelsons Rhus-Tox Cream. Many of these rubs also work by the counter-irritation process.

Ibuprofen is available in a gel form, one called Ibuleve, for example, so that you can apply it directly at the point of pain, where it is quickly absorbed into the skin. It's claimed to be particularly useful for conditions such as backache, rheumatic and muscular pain, as well as sprains and strains. It can be applied up to three times a day, but isn't recommended for children under fourteen or for patients with a history of kidney problems, asthma or aspirin-sensitivity, without getting the advice of their doctor first. It shouldn't be used while pregnant or while breastfeeding.

While bed rest and painkillers are often prescribed particularly in the initial phase of pain caused by back problems, occasionally epidural injections of cortisone can be used to ease severe pain.

HOW TO HANDLE YOUR DOCTOR AND WHEN TO GET HELP

As I've already tried to point out, the back can be one of the most vulnerable points in our bodies from a structural point of view – leading an upright, vertical life tends to put excessive strain upon both bones and joints as well as the muscles and ligaments. This vulnerability can lead to all types of problems needing a variety of treatments.

So, because the causes are so numerous, for a first attack of back pain it is advisable to consult your doctor to rule out the less common causes. It often helps just being assured that there is nothing seriously wrong, even though it may be difficult for your GP to pinpoint the exact problem.

I know that for many people the pain they experience isn't even enough to make them visit their GP, particularly as many sufferers feel that painkillers and rest are likely to be recommended and they can do that for themselves. So when you consider that it's estimated that more than two million people a year visit their GP because of backache, you can appreciate the true extent of back problems.

When you encounter your first attack of back pain, or if the pain is severe and you are in a great deal of discomfort which doesn't ease after a day, I would advise you to see your GP before trying any DIY treatments. He may be able to determine straight away the kind of condition it is (for instance, that it is a *back* problem and not a symptom of another condition, see below) and how successful or otherwise simple treatments will be.

As I've explained earlier, in the case of prolapsed discs, pain is due to pressure from the bulging disc pressing on surrounding nerves, as the discs themselves do not contain any nerves. The amount of pain and other symptoms, such as pins and needles or numbness, will depend on which nerves are affected. But strains and sprains of the back muscles, tendons and ligaments can also cause inflammation and nerve pressure and produce similar, if slightly less intense, pain. So that's why with any back pain, especially a first episode, you should see your doctor to try to establish what exactly is causing the trouble. Don't ignore pins and needles or sensations of numbness. Always get them checked out.

When you consult a doctor, he will have to decide whether the pain is a result of one of the more common mechanical back problems or whether you have an inflammatory arthritis, such as ankylosing spondylitis. A painful back could signify various other health problems from a kidney complaint, a duodenal ulcer, to heart and lung disease or even an infectious disease such as meningitis or shingles, particularly if it is accompanied by a general feeling of being unwell or a raised temperature. So my advice is never ignore back problems.

You can only get the best from your doctor by communicating with him. He will question you carefully and look for certain clues to establish the nature of your problem. So when describing your symptoms first tell him the worst ones and then give brief clear details. It helps if you make sure you explain exactly where the pain is, so he can establish whether, for example, you have a slipped disc with sciatica, which would be pain spreading down your leg due to pressure on the sciatic nerve.

Sometimes we can experience back problems without any apparent reasons, and if this is true in your case then you need to make sure you mention this to the doctor. Half the population go to see their GP at some time in their life because of a back problem, but it's important that when you get to the surgery you explain clearly what your symptoms are and what you think might have caused them.

So make sure you tell your doctor if you've been lifting heavy things, or taking part in some kind of physical activity.

As a very general rule, mechanical back problems mean that you're in more pain when you move around and this seems to ease when you are keeping still or lying in a position that you find comfortable. So tell your doctor what activities make your back pain worse. However, in some cases of sciatica or a prolapsed disc, sufferers say no matter how they position themselves or how still they are, they can get no relief from the pain.

Also try to recall other symptoms: if you've experienced stiffness in your back particularly first thing in the morning, or if you find your pain means you cannot sleep and it's more noticeable and intense when the house is in darkness, the streets are quiet and there's nothing to take your mind off it. Any information of this nature will help your GP make an accurate diagnosis or decide that you need to be referred to a specialist – a rheumatologist, orthopaedic surgeon or a neurosurgeon, a physiotherapist or even an osteopath or chiropractor.

You may or may not be sent for x-ray. Some doctors are not convinced that x-rays of the lumbar spine prove particularly helpful because the small degenerative changes that could show up are more likely to do with the ageing process than any pain we feel in our backs. Also an x-ray is very unlikely to shed much light on a mildly prolapsed disc, for example, as soft tissues such as muscles and ligaments or a bulging disc don't always, directly, show up. But other doctors believe that showing a patient a 'normal' x-ray helps to put their mind at rest and reassure them that there's nothing seriously wrong with them.

And remember: don't be frightened to ask your doctor questions and to go back if your symptoms persist, or if you're worried you may have developed side-effects to your medication, or indeed if you feel the treatment isn't working.

PHYSIOTHERAPY

Many people with back problems find physiotherapy extremely helpful, soothing and relaxing. Physiotherapy can play a vital role in the treatment and management of back problems, especially ankylosing spondylitis where a special exercise programme is essential to keep the patient on the move.

Physiotherapy covers a wide range of techniques and the therapist will usually work out an individual course of treatment for each patient to relieve pain and in some cases to try to improve muscle tone and the range of movements possible.

There are all manner of physiotherapy treatments used these days in addition to exercise programmes. A physiotherapist may use massage, particularly to relieve muscle spasm and help muscles to relax; hot or cold treatments; interferential therapy – a method of using electric current to interrupt the pain–reception network and to reduce inflammation by stimulating circulation; ultrasound – a therapy using sound-waves at high frequencies pointed at an affected area to help relax muscles, reduce inflammation, encourage healing and numb pain; infra-red – a form of deep heat treatment; laser; traction (a means of stretching) in certain cases; and sometimes transcutaneous nerve stimulators (or TENS machines) to relieve back pain.

A TENS machine is a small battery-powered unit which you strap around you, positioning the contact points over the painful area before switching it on. A low frequency signal then stimulates the brain into producing its own natural painkillers, known as endorphins.

It is claimed that fifteen to twenty minutes' use of a TENS machine can overcome the pain for up to twelve hours, depending on the problem. And, although it has to be said that it doesn't work for everybody, three out of four sufferers do find it helpful. It seems to be used more and more these days in the treatment of back pain and to help pregnant women cope with labour pains.

Some companies, such as Neen Pain Management Systems, offer a sale-or-return service for portable TENS machines, but require signed verification from a doctor or physiotherapist that your condition is one that could be helped by the purchase of such a machine. (You can contact Neen Pain on 0362 698966 or write to them at Old Pharmacy Yard, Church Street, East Dereham, Norfolk NR19 1DJ. Or you can ask your doctor or physiotherapist to put you in touch with a supplier. Prices start from around £78.)

TENS is increasingly becoming recognised as a safe and effective means of providing drug-free pain relief, but it should not be used by patients with pacemakers or sufferers from epilepsy. Some specialists also suggest caution when it is used during pregnancy.

In some regions hydrotherapy is offered as part of hospital physiotherapy. This is basically physiotherapy exercises in water, usually in a specially heated pool. The warmth and soothing quality of the water, and also the feeling of weightlessness, helps patients relax their muscles, which in turn improves mobility.

If you've never visited a physiotherapist you can ask your GP to refer you to a physiotherapy clinic attached to a hospital. By the way, some areas provide community physiotherapists to visit patients at home, and some clinics, both in National Health hospitals and private ones, run classes which teach you how to use your body properly and how to understand the workings of your back.

You can also get in touch with a private physiotherapist by contacting the Chartered Society of Physiotherapy (for address see page 100).

FURTHER INVESTIGATIONS

In some cases of back pain – namely when the pain does not subside after a few weeks or recurs frequently – the sufferer will need further investigations and a consultation with a specialist – perhaps with an orthopaedic surgeon, a neurologist or a rheumatologist.

Among possible investigative techniques used these days is the traditional x-ray and newer myelogram – a sophisticated type of x-ray which looks specifically at the spine. The process involves a needle being inserted into your spine and then a dye being injected to pinpoint the problem. It can be a lengthy process, taking up to an hour, and is often quite an uncomfortable experience for the patient.

Newer methods of investigation are proving more popular, such as a CT scan – a type of computerised x-ray – or magnetic resonance imaging (MRI), which combines radiowaves and a magnetic field to create an image. The latter is becoming an extremely useful means of accurately diagnosing what type of disc protrusion a patient has.

SURGERY

Surgery is only necessary in a minority of cases and almost always as a last resort. However it needn't be the major surgery you might expect, since these days new and more delicate techniques are being pioneered. These involve making a very much smaller incision into the back so that only minimal tissue damage is caused and the person recovers much more quickly. When the operation is carried out by a neuro- rather than an orthopaedic surgeon, an operating microscope will more often be used. Opinions are divided on whether this improves the outcome or not – neurosurgeons, not surprisingly, being more in favour than the orthopods.

It's thought that some 11,000 people undergo surgery for back problems per year. This usually involves removing part of the damaged disc, though in some cases the whole disc is removed in an operation called spinal fusion. However this is now performed less and less as it can reduce mobility.

In some cases of prolapsed discs or sciatica the traditional major operation – a laminectomy – is performed. This involves removal of the disc piece that is exerting pressure on the nerve. For the majority of patients this operation will cure the problem at that particular point in the back though in some cases it can lead to problems in neighbouring vertebrae.

In recent years orthopaedic surgeons have become more reluctant to perform laminectomies, particularly for sciatica. Instead microsurgical techniques are used in order to minimise damage to surrounding tissues. This form of surgery can be done in an outpatient clinic without general anaesthetic but more usually in hospital under general anaesthetic.

Microdiscectomy is similar to a laminectomy but enables the surgeon to use a microscope. Also the incision is smaller so the back muscles aren't as disturbed and there is less risk of damage to the delicate structures inside the spinal canal. The operation can take just thirty minutes and patients tend to leave hospital within two or three days as opposed to staying in for a week to ten days as with a laminectomy.

Other techniques being pioneered involve inserting a needle into the disc and aspirating a minute amount from the centre to reduce pressure – technically an automated percutaneous nucleotomy. This is increasingly proving successful.

Surgeons are also pioneering a technique developed in Germany which replaces damaged discs with a type of plastic disc held in place partly by metal plates and partly by the spine itself. A French technique uses four strong metal screws to build a 'cage' around the damaged disc. These are joined with a small piece of special fabric which keeps them rigid for six to nine months when healing takes place. Thereafter it stretches to allow very slight movement.

Another treatment for sciatica due to a protruding or prolapsed disc is called chemonucleolysis or discolysis, which uses an enzyme called papaine – a protein-digesting substance taken from the papaya fruit (often used as a meat tenderiser) to shrink the damaged disc thus relieving pressure on the nerve. The enzyme is injected into the damaged disc using a fine needle, in many units under local anaesthetic. It's a technique that has had a fairly good success rate but it has recently become overshadowed by newer techniques such as those mentioned above.

ALTERNATIVE OR COMPLEMENTARY TREATMENT

Many people with painful back problems have told me that there is nothing much worse than a doctor telling you that you'll have to learn to live with the problem and the pain. This may be the wisest conclusion if the sufferer has tried all the usual options and the symptoms are not severe enough to warrant a major surgical operation. But have *all* possibilities been tried?

I can't honestly say that there is a general consensus on what is the most effective treatment for back problems. The chances of the specific cause of a problem being correctly diagnosed is as low as two out of every ten cases because of the variety of symptoms. And like so many things in life, successful treatment can be a question of trial and error. With most sufferers there is no one remedy that works for them all the time, and perhaps because of this more and more people are turning to alternative forms of treatment. Around half of all people seeking alternative therapy do so because of a back problem, some at the suggestion or with the consent of their GP. But with so little hard evidence to prove that any one treatment is better than another, you pay your money and you take your choice.

There is a growing acknowledgement of the benefits of osteopathy, chiropractic and acupuncture and alternative therapies can bring comfort and relief in many cases. But with severe symptoms – such as the loss of the use of a limb or reflexes, severe pain or an extended length of time before symptoms ease – a consultation with a surgeon is usually the wisest course. The more severe the symptoms, the more likely a GP will be to seek a second opinion.

Alternative therapies may be used effectively in the

treatment of back pain and in this section of the book I discuss some of the options available. But be careful. Make sure that the specialist you see is appropriately qualified. You can always ask your doctor or friends who have found the treatment beneficial to recommend someone. Give them a go but don't spend a fortune persevering with treatments for the sake of it. If it doesn't help you then don't carry on regardless. And do bear in mind that the vast majority of bad backs do in time get better on their own, although this is hard to accept when you're in pain and want relief.

OSTEOPATHY

These days more and more people are going to osteopaths. In fact, osteopathy is probably the 'alternative' therapy most back pain sufferers turn to. It has been described as the most orthodox of the unorthodox therapies and even the Prince of Wales is among its fans, as his presence at the publication of a recent report supporting osteopathy as a therapy confirms.

The General Council and Register of Osteopaths describes the treatment as the 'science of human mechanics' as it's concerned with the structural and mechanical problems of the body.

Osteopaths are keen to point out that the therapy is more than manipulation alone. They use a variety of techniques from soft-tissue massages, to stretching, as well as the high-velocity thrust that most people associate with osteopathy. Actually, this type of manipulation is a minor part of the treatment and some osteopaths rarely if ever use it.

Osteopathic treatment tends to be pleasant and relaxing and tailored to suit the needs of the individual concerned. That's why when you first visit an osteopath you will be thoroughly questioned about your medical history and, in particular when it comes to back pain, just how and when the symptoms first began – so remember to be sure to recall any details whether or not they may seem important to you. As osteopaths are also trained to diagnose and make use of x-rays and blood tests, they will refer you to your doctor if they believe they cannot help you.

The osteopath will examine your spine and look at the way you move around, and don't be surprised if he gives you advice on posture, diet, your lifestyle, or stress, particularly if any of these factors have added to your back problem. You may also be shown special exercises to help mobility or to strengthen your muscles.

Don't entrust yourself to an osteopath without first checking his or her qualifications. You can always phone the Osteopathic Information Service on 071 439 7177.

Osteopathic treatment is not available under the National Health Service but some privately backed schemes will cover the cost, particularly if you've been referred by your GP or consultant. Do check before landing yourself with an unexpected bill.

Margaret, a fifty-eight-year-old housewife, found almost immediate pain relief after four visits to an osteopath. She had damaged her back one morning by twisting as she was getting out of the bath. The painkillers she was prescribed brought little relief and she was beginning to feel quite miserable. Finally her doctor suggested she visit an osteopath, particularly as there was a long waiting list in her area for physiotherapy.

My doctor recommended the osteopath he also visited. I feel it's best to find an alternative practitioner on a personal recommendation.

The treatment was wonderful. It wasn't painful at all – as a matter of fact, it was so gentle that after being there for an hour I wondered when she was going to start. She softly went along my vertebrae with the tips of her fingers, working from the top of my back to my tail and then down my legs. I've never felt so good. I came out smiling – and I hadn't smiled for days.

After the second appointment the pain really eased considerably. I'd never even hesitate to try the treatment again. The money was well worth spending.

The osteopath gave me advice on how to look after my back and on trying to relax more and reduce any stress in my life. I'm very careful about any movements I make now. I bend correctly with back straight and knees bent. I don't lift unnecessary weights. Put it this way, I don't take chances any more.

Sportsmen are often vulnerable to muscle injury and, consequently, back problems, as I've mentioned earlier. More and more of them seem to be turning to osteopaths for help.

Peter, a thirty-year-old accountant and keen sportsman, has had back problems, at both ends of his spine, and been in severe pain playing football and during weight-training.

In my late teens I used to play a lot of football – I was the goalkeeper. I started noticing that as the games wore on the left side of my lower back would become more and more stiff, so stiff sometimes I'd be hobbling around instead of running. At that stage it was more of an annoyance than a hindrance. I used to train a lot. I'd do football training, I also played rugby and did some weight-training. I just thought I was getting tired when I should have had more stamina.

But over a period of about half a dozen games it got worse, until one afternoon I suddenly couldn't move at all. It had been a good game, I'd been playing well, been quite agile, and I'd been making some good saves. I went to pick up the ball and the next thing I remember was being on the ground totally unable to move. I was in such pain and so seized up that I couldn't even get up. I lay there

while the other players decided what to do with me.
I was eventually helped to my feet but still couldn't
walk. It was an hour before I could move a little bit.

When Peter saw his GP he was told he'd torn a muscle
quite badly.

He told me to rest, not to do any exercise and to
sleep on the floor. After a couple of weeks the pain
subsided so I started to do some exercise. I shouldn't
really have done that for at least another two
weeks, until the muscle had fully healed.

Instead for more than six months every time I did
any sport my back would keep going. If I didn't
move around too much I'd be OK but any more
activity and I'd get backache. In fact, it was quite a
few years before the ache eased off completely
when I exercised.

Then, six years ago, Peter developed another problem
with his back, also linked to his exercising routines.

I was lifting some weights above my head when I
heard a crunching noise and once again I couldn't
move. This time, though, I couldn't move my neck
at all, not into any position. It was very frightening
but I told myself it couldn't be that bad because I was
still alive and I could move my arms and legs. I
struggled out to the changing rooms and tried to get
changed, which took ages. I was in such agony I
then went to a hospital casualty department for an
x-ray.

The x-ray showed no fracture but the doctor
there thought I was an interesting case because I
had no sensation in my feet – I didn't even know
he'd been touching my feet!

Again it was decided that Peter's problem was muscular in

origin and he was recommended massage as a means of relieving the pain and stiffness, as massage can help stimulate blood supply to muscles and other tissues in the back.

After a few weeks his neck returned to normal but for the next five years the trouble would recur intermittently.

> My neck would suddenly click again and then go all stiff down my neck and the top of my upper back, across the shoulders. My lower back also began to trouble me again at this time.
>
> Last year I was playing softball when I jumped up to catch the ball. As I did so one of the players running to the base I was guarding happened to clip my feet slightly while I was in the air. My neck felt as if I'd just had a whiplash type of injury. It went rigid and so painful yet again that I thought I really had to get something done about it. I couldn't go on like this.

Peter was recommended an osteopath by a friend, and since visiting her his neck problem hasn't resurfaced.

> She manipulated my neck. She used her hands to twist and turn my head. She made me roll myself into a ball and pressed on the top of my back. As she pressed I could hear crunching, clicking noises – it was horrible! She told me that my muscles had been going into spasm.
>
> I did find osteopathy really helpful and I haven't had any problems since. She really did cure it. She also gave me advice on my lower back and that because I sit at a desk all day long then go straight to the gym I need to make sure I do stretching exercises. It's important to warm up by going on a bike for ten minutes to get the blood circulating before stretching and then doing a work-out.

CHIROPRACTIC

The name chiropractic originates from the Greek 'cheiro' meaning hand and 'praktos' meaning to use. It's the third largest healing profession worldwide, after medicine and dentistry, and is a manipulative therapy similar to osteopathy, though in Britain there are many more qualified osteopaths than chiropractors and osteopathy is much better known.

So what are the differences between them? Both therapies were developed and first used towards the end of the last century but were founded on different philosophies. Chiropractors believed that symptoms stemmed from disorders in the nervous system, whereas osteopaths considered that a poor blood supply to the affected part was responsible. Nowadays these differences have faded and those that do exist are mainly of technique. For instance, chiropractors use x-rays five times more frequently than osteopaths to make a diagnosis and check on progress during treatment. Many chiropractors have x-ray machines on their premises.

Osteopathic treatment tends to include more soft-tissue techniques (various types of massage) and indirect rather than direct ways of adjusting (manipulating) the affected joints. The emphasis in chiropractic is on prevention and adjustment. However there are also many similarities in the methods used and neither treatment includes any form of surgery and very rarely drugs, which greatly enhances their appeal to many people.

Chiropractors believe that most problems occur because of misalignment – or 'subluxation' – of one or more of the vertebrae which, they say, can irritate, pinch or cause pressure on a nerve resulting in pain or symptoms. And since the spine is the body's primary form of support as well as the channel for the spinal cord and the nervous systems, back and spinal difficulties can lead to discomfort and pain in many other parts of the body. For example, pains in your leg can often be the result of a trapped nerve in your back.

Chiropractors and osteopaths aim to realign the bones and reduce nerve irritation mainly through adjustment (manipulation). They also relax muscles in spasm, relieve pain and restore or improve normal movement which, in cases of back problems, can be very beneficial.

Chiropractors believe that for a type of back problem like a slipped disc improvement is made by adjusting the vertebrae to ease pressure on the disc to allow normal movement. For sciatica adjustments are made to the spine and pelvis. Chiropractic can help with low back problems in pregnancy due to the strain on the back caused by the enlarging abdomen without harmful side-effects to mother and baby, as well as ease any back problems caused by a difficult birth.

Other conditions can respond to this type of treatment also, including shoulder and arm pain, pins and needles, hip and knee problems, headaches, even, it is claimed, asthma, period pains and bedwetting.

In suitable cases, therapists say that people of any age, including children, can benefit. At the first visit the practitioner will take a full medical history to look for any underlying causes for the symptoms. The examination may include blood and urine tests and special orthopaedic assessments, as well as x-rays. These careful preliminaries mean that if this type of treatment is agreed upon it is soundly based, and if the therapist considers that manipulation would be unsuitable (as in some forms of arthritis, for example) or conventional medical advice is needed instead, he or she will say so. The chiropractor will also advise, if necessary, on correct posture and seating – common reasons for back or neck pain, especially for office workers – and may suggest other preventive changes in lifestyle.

A common anxiety when deciding whether to try manipulation, and a question I'm often asked, is 'Will it hurt?' The answer is, it may – but usually only briefly and often not at all. Much will depend on how long-standing the problem is and on the tenseness of the muscles – pain is less likely the more relaxed you are, so try not to resist the manipulation.

The techniques used will vary according to the person's age and physique – for example, a frail, elderly lady with back pain will be treated more gently than a robust young man with a rugby injury. As each person is different, an individual treatment programme will be devised. Strength on the part of the therapist is not an important element – success depends on using a carefully controlled force, speed and depth of adjustment learnt over years of training. Usually it is necessary to have a course of treatment lasting several weeks and the therapist may then recommend a maintenance session every few months (just as you have regular check-ups with the dentist) to prevent problems recurring.

Many people say that the symptoms of their back problems have been greatly relieved, or cured, by osteopathy or chiropractic treatment. But manipulation doesn't help when joints are inflamed, in cases of arthritis, for example, and not all problems can be treated by chiropractic. When a chiropractor establishes that the patient has an acute inflammatory disease or rheumatoid arthritis they'll be referred elsewhere. Sudden jerks of the head in someone suffering from rheumatoid arthritis, for example, could be dangerous since the inflamed and weakened tissues and vertebral bones could be further damaged and harm rather than protect the central nervous system, the delicate bundle of nerves running down the centre of the spine.

For some chiropractic is not as successful as they would have hoped. A few find their condition worsens, but this is mainly due to having inadvertently consulted an unqualified practitioner – which is why it is so important to look for a properly trained one, or be referred to one by your GP. Do be sure the chiropractor has the initials 'DC' after his or her name. To become a chiropractor students must follow a four-year full-time course, resulting in a BSc degree in Chiropractic. This is followed by another year's postgraduate course at an established clinic before the student is allowed to apply for membership of the British Chiropractic Association.

Because of the treatment's individuality there is no average length of time for the course of treatment your back problem may need, so don't forget to ask for an estimate of how much the treatment is going to cost so that you can budget for it.

Chiropractic is increasingly becoming recognised as a safe and effective method of treating back problems. A relatively recent study funded by the Medical Research Council has added weight to this, finding that chiropractic treatment was more effective than hospital outpatient therapies for those with chronic or severe back pain. The study even called for the consideration of chiropractic being introduced into NHS practice.

When Gregory, a forty-year-old solicitor, strained his back on a barge holiday he had no hesitation in consulting first an osteopath, then a chiropractor, even though he hadn't seen his GP. He now firmly believes in giving osteopathy or chiropractic a go.

> I could hardly move because of the pain in my back but I didn't even try conventional medicine. I knew that I would have to lie flat on my back for weeks and I simply couldn't afford to do that. I'd got a business to run.
>
> Initially I saw an osteopath who managed to get me upright again. I was still in pain but able to carry on working.
>
> The osteopath was very effective at giving me short-term relief, but I found I had to see him every four to six weeks about the pain in my lower back. I began to think that there had to be a more scientific approach. I wasn't dissatisfied with osteopathy but I was dissatisfied with its long-term effects.

For his next stage of treatment Gregory decided to try chiropractic, which has turned out to be highly effective.

Chiropractic doesn't seem to involve anything dramatic – there's no obvious heaving and pulling. The chiropractor does identify internal muscles that are very tight, particularly muscles in my groin, and when he applies pressure that can be painful.

I've found the treatment enormously effective. Now I go back to keep on top of things and I don't have the regular recurrence of back pain I had before. I still experience the occasional pain but I only need to visit the chiropractor at about ten-week intervals.

ACUPUNCTURE

Acupuncture has been around as a form of treatment in China for five thousand years and these days more and more people in the West are turning to it for a wide variety of ills, particularly back problems. So what is the theory behind it, what does it actually involve and could it help you?

Traditional acupuncture is a 'holistic' form of medicine – a philosophy which not only treats the symptom but also aims to improve the total well-being of the person. Practitioners believe that many physical conditions can be aggravated by, or even due to, emotional stress, unsuitable diet, and other factors. So your first visit to an acupuncturist will probably include detailed questions about your lifestyle and a thorough examination – the tongue is especially important in making a diagnosis so don't be surprised if this is carefully examined!

Acupuncture aims to correct any disharmony within the body – to achieve a balance between positive and negative energy which the Chinese call Yin and Yang. An imbalance, they say, leads to disease. This energy flows along pathways in the body called 'meridians'. These cannot be seen but can be detected using special techniques and can be likened to the nerve pathways known to Western doctors. There are twelve main meridians either side of the body, each related to specific organs such as the heart, liver and stomach. There are also other meridians, such as those used when treating emotional problems like depression and nervousness.

Twelve different pulses on the wrists also relate to the various organs and these, too, are taken into account when the acupuncturist is deciding on treatment.

Each meridian has many points along it in precise positions called 'acupoints'. During acupuncture very fine needles are inserted into several of these points, carefully chosen depending on the problem being treated. However the needles are said to feel no worse than an accidental pin-prick and may be more effective than the alternatives. Probably about eight needles will be used in treatment but it may be anything from one to twenty. They are inserted to varying depths, twirled from time to time and usually left in place for about twenty minutes each session.

It may surprise you that the needles are often inserted in places that appear unrelated to the position of the pain or the symptoms. This is because the points on the meridians can affect parts of the body some distance away and many points interrelate. The outer ear, for example, has a large number of acupoints which correspond to various parts of the body. Sometimes the needles will be slightly heated to add to their effect, and very often, for a painful condition like backache, the acupuncturist will twirl or tap the needles at points at the base of the spine, the inside and back of the legs and even one on the ear, for perhaps as long as forty minutes.

Electroacupuncture is often used but for shorter periods of time. The needles are similar but rather than being manipulated by hand, they are made to vibrate by an electric current from a machine known as an acupunctoscope.

Many studies now show that acupuncture can relieve a wide variety of symptoms and can also help problems such as obesity, giving up smoking and reducing the craving for alcohol and drugs. It is thought to relieve pain partly by stimulating the body's production of natural painkillers called endorphins – in tests raised levels have been detected twenty minutes after treatment. We know that it can also have a calming effect on an over-active gut and using specific acupuncture points on the back has been shown to enlarge the breathing tubes and may help in asthma and chronic bronchitis. Other conditions that can benefit include headaches and migraine, skin problems, arthritis, tinnitus, insomnia, anxiety and depression but no one can predict who will respond and who will not. One study in a general practice showed that 70 per cent of people complaining of various aches and pains in their muscles and bones were likely to be helped by acupuncture.

Acupuncture tends to work in stages. Often the first visit is ineffective but there should be progressive improvement after that. A course of treatment usually involves four to ten sessions and the effect can last six to nine months – sometimes longer. Occasional sessions may then be needed to maintain the benefit. Not all conditions are suitable for acupuncture – serious diseases such as cancer and heart disorders, for example, or anything needing an operation. If in doubt, ask your doctor's advice before deciding to give it a try. He or she may also be able to recommend a practitioner to you.

Sometimes acupuncture can be used in conjunction with conventional medicine to improve the patient's general well-being. There are some practitioners – many GPs for instance – who have done a shortened course in acupuncture, not involving the whole philosophy, and will use it in a limited way, such as to relieve pain.

Always be sure to go to a well-qualified acupuncturist – those with letters after their name such as BAAR or TAS, for example. Any adverse effects should then be most unlikely and you can be sure that the needles used will be properly sterilised. See page 101 for addresses.

Julia, a forty-year-old recently trained reflexologist, has had back problems for the last fourteen years. She's a firm believer in the benefits of acupuncture and feels it is foolish to dismiss alternative treatments without trying them first.

I believe you need to find the things that suit you. When you are in pain it's difficult to be able to sift through the things that can help but it's worth persevering.

Recently I have had four lots of acupuncture, then went on to massage and osteopathy. I found that the acupuncture was good. It generally relaxed me and eased the pain because I'd been feeling so tense. I did feel that I was releasing the blockages in the energy channels. I had some needles in the top of my head and had them in different places in different sessions. The needles were left in place for about half an hour.

It was a shame I had to jump in the car afterwards and drive home. I could have gone to sleep, just knowing there was a possibility of relief made me relaxed.

I was beginning to find that I was holding myself awkwardly just trying to avoid aggravating my back pain. After the first session I was definitely more relaxed and more fluid in my movement. I feel when you are relaxed your body can deal with what's wrong. It hasn't cured the problem but acupuncture has definitely eased it.

THE ALEXANDER TECHNIQUE

The Alexander Technique is a gentle method aimed at relaxing muscles and improving posture by undoing bad sitting and standing habits. As poor posture does indeed contribute to many back problems and backache, the technique can be a good aid to breaking the cycle of bad habit/bad back. Prevention is always better than cure.

The technique was first developed in the 1890s by Frederick Matthias Alexander, an Australian actor and reciter. He became hoarse during performances and so worked out a new approach to balance, posture and movement which resulted in great improvement in his general health.

His technique is a gentle one which helps to relax muscles by teaching the pupil to sit, stand and move gracefully without strain. In this way, so the theory goes, you can rid yourself of the persistent tension that so often causes a variety of problems, particularly backache, headaches, tiredness and depression. Many dance and drama schools teach the technique and it's even becoming popular in sport – the 1990 World Cup Italian football team is said to have used it in training.

The technique teaches you to listen to your body and helps you find ways to change your posture to avoid using effort that just isn't necessary and to stop you slipping back into your old habits of slouching or hunching your shoulders or pulling your head back needlessly. Many people push out their jaw and stretch their neck when getting up from a sitting position instead of using their leg muscles to push them up. Other bad habits can be drawing your chin towards your chest, rounding your shoulders and, at the same time, almost trying to make your body appear shorter. It's surprising how many people do this when they're feeling anxious, or stiffen all their muscles without even knowing it. The technique helps you understand when you are working against your natural poise and allowing your bad habits to take over. It teaches you how to put this understanding into practice, especially when you're under stress.

An Alexander Technique teacher can point out to you tension you weren't even aware of and how you trigger off this tension at the thought of movement, and instructs you on how to prevent this. Most importantly the teacher improves your awareness of your body so that you can recognise tension before it builds to the point of causing muscle pain.

It's very difficult to get across exactly how the technique works and if you are interested it is possibly worth trying a lesson or two to understand what all the fuss is about. Some people find one lesson so relaxing they want to learn more about the technique in order to adapt its teachings into their everyday life.

The Alexander Technique is taught on a one-to-one basis because the teacher needs to place his or her hands on the pupil's body as well as explaining the method. Also different people have different bad habits so treatment needs to be designed to your individual lifestyle. The teacher usually chooses a simple movement, say sitting or standing, to work on. Some time is also spent lying on a table while you are taught how to perfect the technique.

It's beneficial to begin with two or three lessons a week, gradually spacing them out as you acquire the ability to practise on your own. You can discuss alternatives with the teacher if this is impractical. If it does appeal to you, it's generally accepted that you'll need a course of twenty to thirty lessons. Some local authority education centres run group classes. The cost of a lesson is comparable to a session with an osteopath, acupuncturist or other alternative therapist and some teachers will offer an introductory lesson free of charge. Teachers have completed an intensive three-year course approved by the international STAT organisation (Society of Teachers of the Alexander Technique).

Susan, who talked about her back problems in the slipped disc section, see page 19, benefited greatly from micro-surgery three years ago and has also been helped by learning the Alexander Technique.

> I've met so many people who've had surgery and expect everything to be wonderful again imme-diately. Yes, surgery is good but you have to then work at keeping your back well.
>
> In my opinion your back is then naturally going to be weak after surgery. You can't expect wonders. I've tried to strengthen my back by swimming and I've had lessons to swim front crawl properly because my surgeon warned me that breaststroke

wasn't very good for your back, especially when you don't do it properly.

I had a taster lesson of the Alexander Technique and liked it, so I've had quite a few lessons since then. I was amazed at how relaxed it makes me. I've found that being able to relax is half the battle when you are in pain. Feeling tense because of pain just makes the pain even worse. I was taught to do a twenty-minute relaxation routine which I try to do every night before going to bed. I lie for at least twenty minutes with my knees bent up, my hands on my tummy with elbows out wide and feet flat on the floor hip width apart. My head has to be supported by a book – so that it's level with my body, not tilting back or forward. I have to think my back long and wide. It's important to keep your eyes open because you must be able to keep the relaxed feeling you get when you're not relaxing and are aware of what's going on around you. That really helps me.

I've also incorporated the Alexander Technique into my everyday life. I work at an animal rescue centre and even when I'm at work cleaning out kennels, my teacher has shown me how to hold myself in the correct way so that I take any pressure off my back. I think about how I walk and sit so that movements are fluid not jerking. The technique is all about thinking about how you move. I'd definitely recommend giving it a try.

REFLEXOLOGY

The origins of reflexology can be traced back thousands of years and the technique is thought to have been used by the Ancient Egyptians. The art of foot reflexology today was established in the 1930s by an American therapist called Eunice Ingham. Some people believe that this method of treatment can be helpful in alleviating all manner of ailments, from bunions, headaches, insomnia, to vertigo, even high cholesterol and deafness. I have to admit, I'm not entirely convinced it can work for many of these conditions – though I would support their 'cure' for headaches, for example.

Reflexology works on the understanding that there are areas, called reflex points, on the feet and also hands, that match up with each organ, gland and structure of the body – the sole of the foot is thought to represent a map of the body. The spine's reflex point is along the inside edge of both feet which is supposed to be similar in shape to that of the spine. The four arches of the spine – cervical, thoracic, lumbar and sacral – are reflected in the four arches of the feet.

A treatment of reflexology can last around thirty to forty minutes and is likely to involve a variety of massage techniques using the thumb and index finger in addition to a way of rotating the foot, called reflex rotation or pivot-point technique. The technique is a gentle one and many people find it quite pleasurable. It's considered that the main benefit is its powers of relaxation, which can relieve stress and tension. It's also said to improve blood supply and to encourage the unblocking of nerve impulses. Many forms of low back pain can be eased by reflexology, particularly back pain that's related to tension.

SHIATSU

Shiatsu is a Japanese form of therapy meaning 'finger pressure', although it can be applied with other parts of the hand, even with elbows and knees. Apparently, some people who can't bear the thought of needles choose shiatsu instead of acupuncture because of this.

Shiatsu involves pressure on the acupuncture points so that the balance of the body's energy can be restored to promote good health. Like acupuncture there is a variety of shiatsu techniques all linked by a belief in the basic principle – that a vital force, Ki, flows through the body via channels called meridians. Pressure applied to points along the meridians is thought to have a similar effect to the needles of acupuncture. When the balance is upset, the Ki doesn't flow smoothly. Shiatsu involves two main techniques, those of pressure and stretching.

The therapy, it is claimed, eases stress, stiffness and pain as well as improving movements and a person's flexibility. It's also thought to improve circulation, help rid the body of toxins and generally make you feel more relaxed – and you don't need to be ill or in pain to benefit from the technique.

Aches and pains in the back are among the most common problems treated by a shiatsu therapist. A session usually lasts an hour. As well as discussing your medical history the therapist may well ask you to walk around the room so that any posture imbalance can be seen. A course of treatment may involve around five or more sessions.

YOGA

Yoga has been practised in India for centuries as a means of maintaining mental and physical health. It can lead to good posture by teaching you to breathe properly and become flexible and supple. Don't rush into things if you start a yoga class, take things slowly but surely.

THE FELDENKRAIS TECHNIQUE

This is another technique similar to the Alexander Technique in that it is said to promote good health and ease back pain by helping to develop better posture.

SELF-HELP TREATMENT

WHAT YOU CAN BUY

The medical profession and alternative therapists can treat and advise you on your back problem, but the day-to-day management and/or avoidance of any back pain is really up to you. You are the one who must take painkillers or anti-inflammatory medicines as directed; follow exercise programmes; rest as much as you need and try to avoid situations where you needlessly put your back at risk of stress.

In the section Bed Rest and Painkillers (pages 51–5) I discussed the medicines that you may be prescribed by your doctor and the ones you can buy over the counter in pharmacies, shops and even supermarkets. There's quite an array to choose from so be sure to read that section to decide the painkillers that may be most suitable for you.

There are also homoeopathic and herbal remedies for back pain available over the counter. These can sometimes help reduce inflammation and ease muscle spasm. Remedies recommended for back pain are *Aconite*, *Arnica*, *Bryonia*, *Calcarea flourica*, *Nux vomica*, *Rheumasol* and *Rhus tox*. In the New Era range of homoeopathic medicines you can buy tablets for back problems called Sciatica, Neuralgia, Neuritis; Backache, Lumbago, Piles; and Fibrositis and Muscular Pain. Herbal remedies on sale include Potter's Herbal Backache Tablets and Sciargo for sciatica and lumbago.

If you don't like the idea of pills or rubs and liniments, and prefer a more direct means of pain control, home cold treatments can give you some comfort by numbing pain as well as reducing swelling and bruising. For example you can use a packet of frozen peas, protecting your skin by keeping a damp cloth or flannel between you and the packet, or you can simply rub the painful area with ice-cubes. You could also try using an ice-pack from your picnic cold-box.

Heat treatment may be more effective, however, and preferable if you don't like the idea of damp coldness. Warmth from a hot bath, a shower, careful use of an electric blanket, or heat applied with a hot water bottle wrapped in a dry or damp towel (to prevent burning your skin) all help relax muscles and ease pain. After bruising or straining you could try combining the effect of taking a painkiller with warmth from a hot water bottle wrapped in a towel and placed on a painful area, or try a long soak in a warm bath. Generally heat treatment can improve blood circulation, relax muscles and reduce stiffness but is not so good for swelling.

Many back sufferers tell me that they find the new heat pads, which you can buy from the chemist, very helpful. These heat treatments shouldn't be used with liniments or embrocations. Makes available include Robinson Fast Aid Heat Pad which can give more than five hours of deep, relieving warmth. This pad has an adhesive side to hold it in place over the affected area, although the heat pad shouldn't be applied to injured or broken skin, mucous membranes, bruises and skin with a rash or eczema. You should also discontinue use if you develop a rash or if the warmth becomes uncomfortable.

Pharmacies also offer an interesting range of non-drug based products for dealing with aches and pains; among them are Relief-Xtra – small adhesive magnetic discs designed to give magnetic force stimulation to areas of muscle stiffness or tension; the backwarmers with cover; the Dreamland Heating Pad; and the more expensive Omron Pulse Massager which uses low-frequency waves to stimulate nerves and muscles to relieve pain, stiffness and general fatigue (patients with heart disease or those using a pacemaker should not try this product). Then there is the Novasonic Intra-Sonic Transducer which transmits sound-waves to allow treatment to areas that may not respond to conventional massage.

There are back support belts which are designed to support the spinal and abdominal muscles. You can also buy inflatable back supports or Scholl Backease shoe inserts. These special inserts are said to help absorb the impact of walking as it's thought that some back pain may be caused by 'foot shock' due to the non-resistant surfaces we walk on.

Corsets and collars can provide temporary support, perhaps helping you become more mobile and restoring confidence, but corsets should not be used for more than three to four weeks or joints will stiffen up.

Many sufferers find that they get great comfort from talking to other people with back trouble, not only because they then feel they are not alone in their problems, but also because they can discover what self-help measures other people use. The National Back Pain Association is the only national charity for back pain and it does sterling work in funding research, giving sufferers encouragement and offering practical help. It has a network of branches throughout the country. If you'd like to know more about their work their address is listed on page 102.

PREVENTION

While it's true to say that there are many things on the market and many steps you can take yourself to relieve the pain, prevention is far better than cure. I know you'll have heard these words before, but they are worth heeding.

Once you've had a back problem there will often be a weakness that can occur again without warning. Joan, a fifty-four-year-old nurse, has suffered with chronic low back pain for the last six years, probably due to a weakness in her back after suffering two prolapsed discs when she was young. She's well aware of how important prevention is – for those who've already experienced the agonising pain of a back problem as well as for those who haven't.

> Most of the time the pain is like a nagging toothache. I'm so careful not to aggravate the

problem. I know I'd only have to bend incorrectly or turn too quickly and the pain would become unbearable.

Like many back pain sufferers I sleep with a board under my mattress. I've found I can't lie on my back, sleeping on my side is much more comfortable. When I've been in bad pain I've even slept on the floor propped up against a bean bag to give me support.

I'm always thinking about how I move and the consequences of what I'm doing. I always keep my back straight and bend from the knees. I sit upright in a hard chair – I never slump or slouch. If I stand in one position for too long when I'm cooking or making pastry it can hurt my back, so I make sure to change position.

As Joan makes clear, there's no point in returning to all your old bad habits once you've recovered from an episode of back pain.

The Chartered Society of Physiotherapy suggests six golden rules for looking after your back that are well worth remembering. These are: maintain good posture, watch your weight, keep fit, consider your everyday activities, recognise your sporting capabilities and lift wisely. If you try to stick to these guidelines you'll be well on the way to having a better back.

Being overweight definitely aggravates any underlying back pain. You wouldn't dream of carrying a rucksack weighing a couple of stones on your back day and night, yet many people carry that amount of excess weight without ever realising the need to lose it. Excess weight, in itself, doesn't cause back problems but if you have a back 'weakness' it can both trigger and exacerbate it.

Even the most minor stress can add up to severe strain and in some cases can lead to permanent damage. One basic movement to be avoided is standing for a long time, particularly in one position and particularly if the back is slightly bent forward. So often we stand in this way without even realising we are doing it and certainly without realising the strain we're putting on our backs. Typical activities in which we adopt this stance include ironing, washing up or serving at a shop counter. Try not to stay in this position for too long without moving, stretching or sitting down now and then. Stretching or walking around is important because your muscles and ligaments need to get a little exercise – believe me, they weren't designed to hold the same position for a long time.

If you have to stand for a long period either at work or, for example, waiting for a bus, stand with your feet slightly apart so that your weight is evenly distributed. Don't slouch and don't lean to one side, putting more weight on one leg than the other. But don't try to stand too upright either – this in itself is an unnatural position that can put a strain on muscles. Even the way we walk can affect the stress on our backs, since we can develop bad habits without being aware of it. The Alexander Technique, mentioned on page 75, is one way to correct this.

We have to treat our backs with care, which isn't always easy with the busy lives most of us lead. But the worst strain of all that you can inflict on your spine is, as I said earlier, lifting something heavy from floor level and twisting at the same time. About half of all back injuries stem from lifting things incorrectly. When you have to pick up something, do so bending at the knees with a straight back, like a fork-lift truck, rather than bending over from the waist, like a crane. If you must lift something without getting help (and even when you do have help) remember to bend at the knees and lift any heavy object with it held close to the body and the spine kept straight. Don't twist your spine. And what's the point in lifting heavy objects if they can be broken down into smaller pieces or loads? Lifting one box at a time may take longer than three in one go but your back will thank you for it in the long run, I can assure you. If you need to lift things as part of your job always try to use a trolley.

Derek, a forty-eight-year-old personnel officer, has

found that by learning to stand and lift correctly his back problem can be controlled.

> I first hurt my back fifteen years ago. I think it was a combination of lifting things awkwardly combined with playing squash awkwardly – it can be such a violent game. An x-ray showed that my spine was twisted and that one of the vertebrae in my lower back had slipped slightly out of place which consequently pressed on a nerve.
>
> The problem would recur, particularly if I bent over for too long without straightening up quickly and it could then take weeks for the pain to go away.

Over the years Derek has tried osteopathy and chiropractic because he felt his GP offered only painkillers rather than treatment for the condition itself.

> I didn't find osteopathy or chiropractic that beneficial. I know that many people wouldn't agree but I believe everyone's back problem is different. The main benefit from chiropractic was that the chiropractor x-rayed my back and pointed out the problem to me. This made the message hit home that I needed to rest instead of struggline back to work.

If Derek injures his back he can be in excruciating pain for weeks so he tries to avoid situations where he might jerk his back violently.

> These days I don't tend to injure it, I just cause a dull ache. That happens usually when I've been bending over too much or stretching, say if I'm up a ladder cutting creepers at the front of the house. I try not to over-stretch but sometimes there are jobs that have to be done.
>
> I find usually I hurt my back when I'm helping

someone else – when pride gets in the way. I don't mind asking my wife or family to help me do something but if the girls at work want a desk moving I'm too embarrassed to say that I can't do it! So I do foolish things sometimes and it then takes me weeks to recover.

Derek also joined a health club in order to keep his back problem under control.

I thought when I first joined that I wouldn't be able to use much of the equipment in the gym because of my back. But I had a proper fitness assessment and found that with proper advice I could use most of it. Generally speaking I've found that it helps me to keep my body supple which seems to help my back. Improving my suppleness helps me more than resting. If I rest too long in one position that aggravates my back.

I do back exercises each morning involving bending and stretching which I was shown by a physiotherapist I was referred to through the gym. She drew attention to the bad habits I'd developed in relation to posture. Looking back at photographs of me as a child I developed the habit of standing with a distended stomach and with my bottom sticking out, which puts a strain on the spine. This strain wasn't helped by drinking beer either!

She thought it would take me six months to overcome my inherent postural problems. The physiotherapist suggested that if I learned how to stand properly, combined with regular exercises, it would help, and it has.

AT HOME AND AT WORK

As well as following advice on posture and avoiding the activities that aggravate your back problem, it's advisable to take a look around your home to find ways of removing potential trouble spots. Examine your furniture, for instance. After a hard day at the office or once the kids have finally gone to bed, I know only too well that the first thing you want to do is flop into an armchair or lounge on the sofa. Yet there's not much worse for putting stress on the lower part of your back. (And while I've mentioned children, they are one of the worst culprits for flopping in front of the television without any support for their still growing backs.) Soft comfortable chairs do tend to encourage a slouching position, so the best chair is one that helps you sit upright and not become a couch potato! If your sofa or armchair doesn't give you the support you need, putting a cushion in the small of your back will help. There are specially shaped chairs available on the market designed to promote good posture and you may feel investing in one of these worth a try.

Beds are important, too. As we spend a third of our lives in bed, we need one that supports the body. For this reason a well-sprung mattress is essential, particularly if you are overweight. As we've seen, for people liable to back pain, a firm board placed under the mattress will provide some temporary extra support and may be helpful. Don't ignore the quality of your bed or the signs of wear and tear. Beds shouldn't be expected to last a lifetime. You need to take advice from a reputable retailer who sells quality beds and buy the best one you can afford.

There's no point using three pillows to rest your head on when one will suffice. Too many can cause the neck to twist, putting pressure on the spine.

We may spend a large part of our lives in bed but many of us also spend a lot of our time in the kitchen. Here, too, you could become the victim of a badly planned work area. And it only takes some simple common sense to avoid a good proportion of basic mechanical back problems.

It's important to make sure your kitchen worktops are fitted at the right height so that you avoid stooping over them when preparing food. If you find your worktops are too high you could sit on a chair or a higher level stool so you avoid leaning over when you're preparing food. Put items which are used the least in cupboards that aren't quite so accessible, which would leave the more accessible space free for anything in constant use, from cutlery to crockery to foodstuffs. You don't have to bend and stretch every five minutes when preparing meals.

If you can, try to use an eye-level oven to prevent you stooping to put food in or take heavy casseroles out. Avoid bending and stretching by kneeling down on the floor to load or unload a washing machine, tumble drier or dishwasher. Washed crockery can be placed on the worktop above the machine. When the dishwasher is unloaded completely, you can then stand to put away the dishes.

Look at your bathroom, too. Leaning over a washbasin or the bath to wash your hair can really put undue strain on your back. Try to wash your hair in the shower instead, or if you don't have a shower or don't like taking one, wash your hair when you're having a bath using an inexpensive plastic or rubber shower spray which you can push on to your bath taps. If you must wash your hair over a basin, try to keep the bottom of your back curved inwards and don't let your shoulders become too rounded.

You should think about your back when you're doing housework. I know of a midwife who coped remarkably with the stresses and strains of delivering babies but pulled a back muscle so badly while changing a duvet cover she needed a whole week off work. To save that happening to you here's a useful tip when you're changing sheets or making a bed: kneel down at the side of the bed to tuck in sheets rather than over-stretching those back muscles. And don't try to turn heavy mattresses on your own. When changing a duvet cover it's helpful to put clothes pegs on the top two corners of the outside of the cover to keep the duvet itself in place while you pull the cover down to the other corners.

When it comes to using a vacuum cleaner, push it backwards and forwards in front of you. Don't twist your spine by moving it diagonally from side to side. When the time comes for a new one, try to buy a model that is quite lightweight.

Even hanging washing on a clothes line can be made less troublesome. Make sure you lower your washing line to a height that means you don't have to stand on tiptoe to peg out the clothes.

Ironing can be made easier by stopping and moving around for a while, and if standing for too long makes your back ache when you are doing the ironing or washing up, you can always raise one foot on a stool to ease the strain. Or you can open the cupboard door under your sink and rest your foot on the cupboard floor. This is especially helpful for pregnant women.

Try to avoid carpets and rugs becoming loose around the house. Tripping and slipping can lead to back problems because of the jarring action on the spine. If you have children try to tidy toys away. They're easy to trip over and you may fall on them awkwardly.

At work, think about what you do. Nurses should always try to lift patients correctly. Office workers should make sure that chairs are the right height for the desk or table at which they are sitting. Typists' chairs should support the lumbar spine and allow the feet to rest flat on the floor with the knees bent at right angles. If you use a keyboard try to keep your elbows also bent at right angles. Don't type with your arms outstretched with your chair far away from your desk.

Driving to and from work, as well as during leisure time, is another area for potential problems. A correct seating position when you're driving is important for avoiding back problems and one that can be forgotten about when you're concentrating on city traffic jams or negotiating a winding country road. Just as when you're relaxing, slouching should be avoided. You should sit supported, upright and straight-backed, with your legs stretched out rather than having your knees knocking the steering wheel. Don't drive for long periods. If you are able to, try to stop, get out of the car and stretch your legs, even if only for a short while. You might also find back supports that fit into a car seat helpful.

Gardening isn't simply relaxation, as all keen gardeners will agree. It's often very hard work and a common cause of back trouble. The Chartered Society of Physiotherapy advises that before you garden, and especially in cold weather, you must warm up your muscles – for example, stretching your back a few times to limber up.

It helps to kneel down when you're planting – use knee-pads or a kneeler. Also try not to jerk your back with sudden movements such as pulling out a shrub or weeds too suddenly. Use tools that have long handles so that you can stand with your back upright and straight rather than bending over to reach the far side of a flower bed. If you use a wheelbarrow, keep your back straight and bend your knees when you lift it. And don't overdo it – no matter how many weeds there are! Pace yourself.

EXERCISE

A survey by the Sports Council and the Health Education Authority has revealed that three-quarters of all adults don't take enough exercise, so it's hardly surprising that back problems are on the increase.

Exercising helps you lose weight, keeps you in trim, strengthens your muscles (particularly helpful for avoiding back problems) and so increases your stamina, and helps maintain a healthy heart. It also improves your suppleness and is a good way of working stress out of your system. And remember, exercise can be something as simple as going for a brisk walk. Cycling too can play an important part in keeping the muscles and ligaments in good tone and gentle jogging is also beneficial, though best done with good-quality shock-absorbing shoes and on grass rather than hard roads.

But bear in mind that moderation in all things is better than extremes. If you want to protect your back start off exercising slowly and gently. Don't believe those words 'No Pain, No Gain.' Little and often is far better.

Don't do sit-ups or touch your toes, especially when keeping your legs straight. Just lifting your head to look at the tips of your toes while lying on your back will tighten and strengthen your tummy muscles and will help your back at other times. You should keep your back flat on the floor the whole time and not move at all so that it remains comfortable.

After a bad attack of back pain, and once you're beginning to feel better, special exercises designed for you by a physiotherapist will usually speed up recovery and help prevent a relapse. Sometimes these exercises include lying face down and raising your head and shoulders, or raising your head and shoulders with your hands behind your head; or on your hands and knees raising first one leg then the other. To do more than this, it really is wise to take personal advice.

Other simple exercises recommended by the Chartered Society of Physiotherapy, to be done from five to fifteen times a day, include rolling your knees from side to side when lying on your back with your legs bent. Or gently rocking your pelvis first to flatten the hollow in your spine and then increase it. Or, when lying on your front with a pillow under your tummy, lifting first one leg then the other, keeping them straight from the hip. Relax between each lift. When standing you could try placing your feet apart and swinging both arms to the left and right. And if any exercise causes you pain, don't do it. If you've had a bad back recently you really should check with your physiotherapist before starting any exercise programme.

If you regularly feel stiffness or a tautness in your neck, shoulders and upper back at the end of a hard day's work, relaxation as well as exercise could be the thing for you. There's nothing quite like stress for causing muscle tension which isn't only unpleasant and uncomfortable in itself, but can also exert a strain on your joints. When you can feel yourself knotting up, work your way up or down your body, tensing and then relaxing your muscles as you go. Slow deep breathing, while thinking about those breaths, can also calm the nerves and tension.

Swimming is an excellent way of improving muscle tone in a weight and gravity-free setting. There's even an Association for Swimming Therapy which may be able to put you in touch with groups in your area if you don't fancy swimming on your own or prefer to do it in a more 'sociable' setting (see page 99 for address).

Swimming is good for relaxing, too. And some people with back problems are quite convinced that it has kept them on the move and fit. Frances, a sixty-two-year-old housewife, has endured crippling low back pain for more than forty years, since she was a trainee nurse in fact, and strongly believes swimming has helped keep her mobile.

> In those days nurses weren't allowed to be ill. I was on a heavy, male surgical ward and was very busy. But people's attitudes were that we all had backache as nurses and you were supposed to carry on in the hope that it would go eventually. Some days I was in such pain and had such stiffness that I had to get up at five in the morning to be able to put on my uniform in time to be on duty at seven-thirty.

Frances's nursing days were the start of bouts of severe back pain that gradually increased in frequency and severity and her problems have only been added to recently when she discovered that she also has osteoporosis. 'I was always told in the past that I had a slipped disc which would heal in time and would right itself.' By the time she was thirty-nine, she had a laminectomy which revealed a severely damaged sciatic nerve.

> I was in agony after the operation but I do think it

helped me. There have been times when I've felt that doctors didn't really want to know about my back problems and it was me who forced myself to carry on.

I came to know that in my case my back didn't 'go' out of the blue. I'd have warning signs a few weeks before. My neck would stiffen, my fingers would feel numb. I'd get sciatica or I'd have slight backache. But when it happens so regularly you tend to switch off and think, 'Oh, my back can't possibly go now, I've got a wedding to go to!'

Swimming I have to say has been of great help to me. I'm a great believer in it as a means of keeping fit. It's so important to keep moving. If you feel well and positive the pain doesn't get to you so much.

It helps even if you just swim a width of the pool. The next time you go you'll be able to do a little more. I've found that although there's always a tendency to do breaststroke, doing backstroke has been more beneficial for me. I think it's because when I do breaststroke my head tends to stick up out of the water and then hurts my neck a little. Doing backstroke doesn't put any strain on the neck.

If you don't like swimming backstroke you can always try front crawl. If you really prefer breaststroke try to keep your head in line with your body.

Over the years Frances has adopted several self-help measures. She has found heat pads particularly useful.

If you can't sleep at night, don't just lie there thinking about the pain, get up, have a hot drink, and apply heat to your back to soothe it. I've found that really helpful, as well as placing a pillow under my knees which helps keep the bottom of my spine straight and brings great relief.

Other sufferers find that they have more comfort and

less pain when they lie on their side. If this is more suitable for you, don't rest the knee of your upper leg on the mattress because it can twist your back. You can lie on your side with a pillow between your knees to stop this happening – a tip many pregnant women find helpful.

> Another thing I even take on holiday is a home-made neck pillow to help me sleep in a comfortable position. I cut a pair of tights off at the knees, stuff them with lots of old tights and tie the ends to make a kind of sausage shape with two legs coming down from it. It's very good for supporting your neck although if you do take it on holiday I'd put it in your suitcase during the day in case the chambermaid wonders what on earth it is!

While we're on the subject of exercise, what about sex and back pain? For either a man or a women with back problems, the best position is for them to be flat on their back with their partner on top.

A good preventative measure when it comes to exercise and back problems is to make sure you do a gentle warm-up routine before taking part in sport, and never carry on if your back hurts during a game or match. Pain is usually a sign that something is wrong and should be regarded as a warning. If you do ignore pain when you're playing sport you're likely to cause further damage.

Not warming up before a game of netball or tennis, when she knew she was in pain, meant that Margaret, a thirty-two-year-old information specialist, has had intermittent upper back problems for the past seven years. Fortunately, by taking several self-help steps she can now control her back problems.

> I hadn't even played netball for five years and went straight into the game without warming up. My muscles were cold and I was bending a lot to pick up the ball. I was fine while I was playing but two hours

later I was in such pain I had to clutch my back to relieve it. I had such pressure on my chest I thought I was having a heart attack. I had shooting pains in my chest and I couldn't get my breath.

I had a pain in my upper back in the centre muscle right near the spine. But I didn't associate the back pain as the problem at the time because most of the pain was at the front of my body under my arm and around my rib cage.

A friend told me it was likely that I'd pulled a muscle in my back.

For the next three nights I slept on the living-room floor. I couldn't sleep in my bed. It was too soft and just aggravated the pain I was in. On the floor I could arch my back slightly which seemed to ease it.

The pain then subsided and Margaret thought no more about it. But three months later the same thing happened again, this time when Margaret was doing some DIY.

I had just moved into a flat and I was pulling off ceiling tiles in the living room. I was on a ladder, with my neck straining upwards looking at the ceiling and I was scraping the tiles off with my right arm. Again, at the time I had no discomfort. But two days later I woke up at three in the morning feeling as if I was having a heart attack with the same shooting pains in my chest.

I was feeling really panicky. I got up and I found that by moving around the pain eased. The pain was so bad that time that it lasted for a couple of weeks. I dreaded waking up in the morning. If I lay still in one position I would be OK. Moving to get out of bed was so painful, yet once I was up and moving around the pain would lessen.

Like so many people Margaret tried to ignore the discomfort and once she began to feel better started playing tennis.

Each time I served I was in agony, but I clutched my side and carried on regardless. This time I saw my doctor who told me that I had indeed pulled a back muscle. He gave me anti-inflammatory tablets which helped a bit. He advised me to lie on my back and arch my back to ease the strain on my muscle.

Sometimes tension, anxiety or mental stress can increase the body's muscle tone to the extent that it triggers off an attack or makes an attack of back pain even worse. Margaret soon noticed that her back problem reappeared when she was under a lot of stress at work, and now the pain affected her neck too. 'I felt as if I had a lump in my throat and I could hardly turn my head to the right-hand side. A friend recommended I see a physiotherapist. Physiotherapy proved useful, not just in terms of immediate pain relief but also because of the advice given on looking after her back.

The physiotherapist found that the third vertebrae down seemed inflamed and that I had a trapped nerve in my neck. She gave me ultrasound treatment and manipulated the vertebrae. She also gave me a good massage and explained a little of the Alexander Technique. She'd noticed that I was straining my neck all the time, particularly when I stood up from sitting on a chair.

My posture was terrible anyway. I never stood up properly and was always round-shouldered.

Margaret was given a neck collar to wear as a temporary measure. She found this very helpful and still uses it when under stress.

The physiotherapist wasn't that keen for me to have it because it meant that the collar was doing the work supporting the neck and not me. But she knew I was in a lot of pain and agreed that it could help me if I only wore it for an hour or so a day. I found it marvellous and still use it when I feel my neck seizing up. I'm not the sort to lose my temper or scream and shout. I'm sure if I could do that my neck wouldn't tense up so much. Sometimes I feel as if a short, sharp electric current is running through my neck and then suddenly it's gone. I get twinges in my neck even when I'm not under stress.

Margaret could see a pattern emerging. She would hurt her back without realising it and then a couple of days later she'd feel the muscle spasm.

On one occasion I picked up my boyfriend and threw him on the bed as a joke. A few days later I woke up and the same stabbing pains appeared in my chest. This time I had to have a week off work it was so bad. My doctor said he could see the back muscle protruding it was so inflamed. And it's always the same muscle around the bottom of my shoulder blades that gives me trouble.

He suggested I try to strengthen my back muscles by swimming. That has worked well. I have also bought an orthopaedic mattress and a cushion to support my back when I'm driving. I try to be careful about my posture. At work I try to sit with my legs apart, my feet flat on the floor and my back straight. When I stand I try to pull up from my thighs rather than from my neck.

I still play netball and before playing I often use a warming muscle spray or a pre-sport rub, and now I'm very careful to spend at least ten minutes warming up before I do any exercise.

So remember, regular exercise and a little thought everyday about how we use (and abuse) our backs can do so much to prevent painful and immobilising back problems.

HELPFUL ADDRESSES

ARC, Arthritis and Rheumatism Council for Research, Copeman House, St Mary's Court, St Mary's Gate, Chesterfield, Derbyshire S41 7TD. Tel: 0246 558033. The ARC is the only national charity in the UK raising money solely to further research and knowledge into rheumatic disease. It relies entirely on voluntary contributions yet still manages to raise more than £10 million a year. It also produces many informative and helpful leaflets on all aspects of arthritis in addition to a lively magazine called *Arthritis Research Today*.

Arthritis Care, 18 Stephenson Way, London NW1 2HD. Tel: 071 916 1500. Arthritis Care is a national voluntary organisation which provides information, advice and help by letter and phone (either on the main number or on the helpline 0800 289170, calls free of charge on weekday afternoons). It campaigns for greater public awareness of the needs and problems associated with arthritis. It runs specially equipped holiday centres, self-catering holiday units and a residential home for those who are very disabled. It also provides regular meetings of more than five hundred local branches.

Young Arthritis Care is a section of Arthritis Care and is a self-help support group run by and for all young people with arthritis – anybody up to the age of forty-five.

Association for Swimming Therapy, c/o Ted Cowan, 4 Oak Street, Shrewsbury SY3 7RH. Tel: 0743 344393. Swimming for people with disabilities. About two hundred clubs are affiliated to the association. To find out if there's one near you contact the association.

British Chiropractic Association, Premier House, 10 Greycoat Place, London SW1P 1SB. Tel: 071 222 8866. The association maintains a register of all qualified chiropractors in membership, which is limited exclusively to graduates of recognised chiropractic colleges. The Anglo-European College of Chiropractic and the colleges affiliated to the Council on Chiropractic Education, the

government-recognised accrediting agency for chiropractic education in the United States, are the colleges recognised by the
association.

The register of members of the British Chiropractic Association
is published to provide the public with the names of chiropractors
whose training and ethical conduct can be relied on. All these
chiropractors have graduated with the following qualifications:
DC, B.App. Sc(Chiro), BSc Chiropractic or BSc Chiropractic DC.
For a copy of the register and further information contact the
association.

British Homoeopathic Association, 27a Devonshire Street, London W1N 1RJ. Tel: 071 935 2163. For books, advice, information
and a list of practitioners.

Chartered Society of Physiotherapy, 14 Bedford Row, London
WC1R 4ED. Tel: 071 242 1941. For further information on
physiotherapy and also private practice physiotherapists.

College of Occupational Therapists, 6–8 Marshalsea Road,
Southwark, London SE1 1HL. Tel: 071 357 6480. Occupational
therapy isn't all fluffy toy-making and basket-weaving as some
people might think. An occupational therapist can help educate
and encourage someone who has severe back pain or who has
become disabled because of a back problem, by identifying both
strengths and weaknesses, by building on things you can do and
working out ways round those you can't. Occupational therapists
are keen to help you reach and maintain as much independence as
possible.

Your GP can put you in touch with an occupational therapist, or
you could be referred to one as part of hospital treatment to advise
you on all manner of equipment to help you cope with day-to-day
life. You can contact the college for information on a private
practice register. An occupational therapist can also visit your
workplace to suggest improvements there. Together you can
tackle a particular problem and work out ways to overcome the
limitations placed on you by your condition. An occupational
therapist will talk to you about how you're coping and will listen to
your problems.

Council for Acupuncture, 179 Gloucester Place, London NW1 DX. Tel: 071 724 5756. Send £2 and a large SAE for a directory of British acupuncturists.

DIAL Disablement – a local information and advice line. The DIAL service can provide information about local services including the possibility of local suppliers who loan or sell equipment. Look under the 'Disabled – amenities and information' section in your *Yellow Pages* phone directory for such a service in your area.

Disabled Living Foundation, 380–84 Harrow Road, London SW9 2HU. Tel: 071 289 6111. The foundation is a national charity and provides practical advice and information in particular on equipment for disabled people and their carers. It runs an equipment centre in London for people to view (open 9–5, Mondays to Fridays). Viewing is by appointment and many people find that an appointment with one of the centre's staff is extremely helpful. The centre isn't a shop but offers impartial advice on the equipment on the market. Contact the foundation by letter or by ringing the above number and ask for the Information Service.

General Council and Register of Osteopaths, 56 London Street, Reading, Berkshire RG1 4SQ. Tel: 0734 576585 for names and addresses of registered osteopaths in your area.

Institute for Complementary Medicine, PO Box 194, London SE16 1Q2. Tel: 071 237 5165. Send a large SAE and a clear indication on what kind of information you'd like and on what subject. The institute holds the British register of complementary practitioners and can also give advice on training and courses.

NASS National Ankylosing Spondylitis Society, 5 Grosvenor Crescent, London SW1X 7ER. Tel: 071 235 9585. The society has around sixty groups throughout the country, usually meeting one evening a week in a hospital for group physiotherapy. It also provides book lists, publications, also a cassette of a twenty-minute programme of physiotherapy exercises as well as producing a twice-yearly newsletter containing articles by doctors and sufferers on different aspects of the disease.

National Back Pain Association, 31–3 Park Road, Teddington, Middlesex TW11 0AB. Tel: 081 977 5474. The association provides all kinds of information on back problems, from the kinds of treatment available to how exercise can help. It funds research currently totalling almost £100,000, covering rheumatology, osteopathy and epidemiology and is the only national charity devoted to back pain. It also has a small network of branches.

National Osteoporosis Society, PO Box 10, Radstock, Bath BA3 3YB. Tel: 0761 32472. A registered charity which works to give women the opportunity to enjoy the last third of their lives without the pain and deformity of osteoporosis. It provides support and can put you in touch with self-help groups in your area as well as a treatment centre for osteoporosis near you.

RADAR Royal Association for Disability and Rehabilitation, 25 Mortimer Street, London W1N 8AB. Tel: 071 637 5400. This organisation campaigns for, among other things, the removal of barriers to disabled people be they architectural, economic or just people's attitudes. You can ring its general advice line for information on entitlement to services, aid and equipment or housing, for example. Call the above number and ask for the information department.

Society of Teachers of the Alexander Technique (STAT), 20 London House, 266 Fulham Road, London SW10 9EL. Tel: 071 351 0828. For more information or a list of around six hundred specialist teachers who have taken a three-year training course approved by the society you can write to STAT enclosing an SAE.

The government's Patient's Charter has resulted in the setting up of Regional Health Information Services to provide information about waiting lists (extremely useful if you are awaiting surgery for a back problem), NHS services, self-help groups and common illnesses.

East Anglia, East Anglian Healthlink. Tel: 0345 678 333.

Mersey, Healthwise. Tel: 0800 838 909.

North East Thames, Health Information Service (managed by College of Health). Tel: 0345 678 444.

North Western, Patients' Advice Bureau. Tel: 0345 678 888.

North West Thames, Health Information Service. Tel: 0345 678 400.

Northern, Health Info North. Tel: 0345 678 100.

Oxford, Health Info Line. Tel: 0345 678 700.

Pan Thames, Waiting List Helpline. Tel: 0345 678 150.

South East Thames, Health Directory. Tel: 0345 678 500.

South Western Region, Open Health. Tel: 0345 678 777.

South West Thames, SW Thames Health Information.
   Tel: 0345 678 555.

Trent, Trent Healthline. Tel: 0345 678 300.

Wessex, Wessex Health Information (managed by the charity Heal for Health Trust). Tel: 0345 678 679.

West Midlands, Midlands Health Point. Tel: 0345 678 800.

Yorkshire, Healthbox. Tel: 0345 678 200.

In addition to these regional health information services there's also an indpendent charity called the Help for Health Trust (tel: 0962 849100). It was established by Wessex Regional Health Authority and provides information to the people of Hampshire, Isle of Wight, Dorset, Wiltshire and the Bath area. The trust says it helps people to become active partners in their own health care by providing them with the information they need to make healthy choices.

AUSTRALIA

The Arthritics Foundation of Australia, National Office, Suite 421, Wingello House, Angel Place, Sydney 2000. Tel: 02-221-2456 Funds research on arthritis and other rheumatic diseases. Has affiliated organisations all over Australia for arthritic sufferers.

Australasian Council on Chiropractic and Osteopathic Education Ltd, 941 Neopean Highway, Mornington, Victoria 3931.
Tel: 059-75 35 46

AFONTA (Australian Federation of Natural Therapy Associations), 8 Thorp Road, Woronora, New South Wales 2232.
Tel: 02-521-2063

Australian Osteopathic Association, 2 Hillside Parade, Gleniris 3146. Tel: 03 889 6765

The Australian Physiotherapy Association, 141 St George's Road, North Fitzroy, Victoria 3068. Tel: 03-482-1044

Osteoporosis Foundation of Australia Inc, 100 Miller Street, 27th Floor, North Sydney 2060. Tel: 02-957-5162

CANADA

Ankylosing Spondylitis Association of British Colombia, c/o Arthritis Society, 895 W 10th Avenue, Vancouver, British Colombia V55 1L7.

The Arthritic's Society, 250 Bloor Street East, Suite 401, Toronto M4W 3P2. Tel: 416-967-1414

The Canadian Physiotherapy Association, 890 Yonge Street (9th floor), Toronto, Ontario M4W 3P4. Tel: 416-924-5312

Manitoba Ankylosing Spondylitis Association, Mr Lorne Ferley, 19 Carolyn Bay, Winnipeg, Manitoba R2J 2Z3. Tel: 204-256-5320

Ontario Spondylitis Association, Mr Nils Linholm, 250 Bloor St East, Suite 401, Toronto, Ontario M4W 3P2. Tel: 416-967-1414

Osteoporosis Society of Canada, Suite 502, 76 St Claire Avenue West, Toronto. Tel: 416-922-1358

Osteoporosis Ottawa, 220-1320 Richmond Road, Ottawa. Tel: 613-596-9374

Osteoporosis Society of British Colombia, 203-2182 West 12th Avenue, Vancouver. Tel: 604-731-4997.

INDEX